T0196449

BOOST YOUR
CHILD'S
ACADEMIC
SUCCESS

BOOST YOUR CHILD'S ACADEMIC SUCCESS

121 STRATEGIES

Marshena McCoy-Williams, Ed.D.

BOOST YOUR CHILD'S ACADEMIC SUCCESS
121 STRATEGIES

Copyright © 2016 Marshena McCoy-Williams, Ed.D.

All rights reserved. No part of this book may be used or reproduced by any means, graphic, electronic, or mechanical, including photocopying, recording, taping or by any information storage retrieval system without the written permission of the author except in the case of brief quotations embodied in critical articles and reviews.

iUniverse books may be ordered through booksellers or by contacting:

iUniverse
1663 Liberty Drive
Bloomington, IN 47403
www.iuniverse.com
1-800-Authors (1-800-288-4677)

Because of the dynamic nature of the Internet, any web addresses or links contained in this book may have changed since publication and may no longer be valid. The views expressed in this work are solely those of the author and do not necessarily reflect the views of the publisher, and the publisher hereby disclaims any responsibility for them.

Any people depicted in stock imagery provided by Thinkstock are models, and such images are being used for illustrative purposes only.
Certain stock imagery © Thinkstock.

ISBN: 978-1-4917-9619-1 (sc)
ISBN: 978-1-4917-9621-4 (e)

Library of Congress Control Number: 2016907040

Print information available on the last page.

iUniverse rev. date: 10/10/2016

To my children, Daune, Christopher, and Bernard, and to my grandchildren, Serenity, Jaimee, Christopher Jr., Sky, Neil Jr., Benjamin, and Rimica.

CONTENTS

PREFACE

I first met Earl Washington when his daughter, Eureka—then in her first year at Bennett College—was being inducted into the Bennett Scholars Program, the college's honors program, of which I was the director. Years later, Mr. Washington and I would meet again at my wedding to Lut Williams, one of his closest friends.

Mr. Washington, whom I respectfully call Brother Earl, owned a restaurant for many years and is also a painter. My husband arranged for him to paint Smart Kids TLC (SKTLC), my tutoring and learning center in Greensboro, North Carolina. After completing the job, Brother Earl paid me a visit. He said, "I don't mean any harm, but you have an obligation to write. What you are teaching these children and their parents you must make known to others. You understand children, and you understand parents; you take something that happens or is said and turn it into a lesson. You put compassion into your teaching. I listened to you get those boys to think about the impact of their behaviors on others. I heard you tell parents to have their children drink water before a test and why [see chapter 1, #4]. Children and parents don't know these things. You must write." He then warned me that he would call me each and every month until I agreed to do so. I smiled.

At some point, I shared with him a story about a mom whose daughter was failing. A teacher had suggested the girl was mentally challenged and incapable of learning. The mother admitted that this child did take longer "to catch on" than her older daughter, but she did not accept the teacher's conclusion. Our SKTLC assessment, which we administer to every incoming student, revealed that this middle school child had deficiencies in reading. There was no inability to think or learn. After two years of instruction, at age fourteen, she was accepted to a middle college—reportedly as the youngest in her math class—and earned the highest grades in all of her classes.

Brother Earl responded by saying, "You have a moral obligation to write!"

Proud parents prep their alert, rambunctious, bright-eyed youngsters for school, taking and sending pictures to grandparents, who beam and brag about their cute, darling, smart little ones. They all have high expectations because of their children's many ingenious sayings and surprising abilities. Never, not even in nightmares, do they imagine that their children could exhibit the behavioral or learning problems described by teachers. As one upper-class yet downcast father asked in reference to his daughter's performance on high-stakes standardized tests, "How can a child be smart one day and dumb the next? I don't understand it." Getting a child through school becomes a harrowing experience for many parents, even those whose children escape the commonly known below-grade statistics.

As I reflected on the many stories I'd heard from frightened parents, it became clearer to me that Brother Earl was right; as I thought about the increasing number of children brought to SKTLC who'd been retained, threatened with retention, or labeled, an emotion inside began to grow in intensity. It was outrage— pure outrage at the trauma public and private schools inflict upon millions of parents who worry, fret, and lose sleep over the difficult futures their children could face because of inadequate education. My anger surged as I recalled fathers breaking down and crying with relief upon hearing their daughters had no learning disabilities and could learn at levels beyond their imaginations. Dozens of times, SKTLC has plucked boys and girls from the well-worn paths to prison and vulnerability.

Many children coming to SKTLC have academic problems caused by a pervasive tenet that the majority of schoolchildren are average in intelligence. This dictates low expectations for most of our students. Teachers and administrators are also trapped in a system that seems to curb their creativity and ability to successfully teach.

My thoughts refocused on the pained and hurt expressions on the faces of the hundreds of parents who, for over two and a half decades, have been bringing to SKTLC their children described as "throwaways" or "uneducable" by public, private, and charter schools. It is those parents—with their care and concern for their children, their previous experiences with their children's intelligence, and their belief that their children were capable of learning—who made me write. They need help. Brother Earl was right.

Brother Earl's call came every week like clockwork as he checked on the manuscript's status and reminded me of useful information to pass on. He promised he would not stop until the book was off the press, and he kept his promise.

ACKNOWLEDGMENTS

To the many, many people over the years who have urged me to write at least one book that shares the traditional and nontraditional strategies used to teach and tutor in Smart Kids, Inc., and Smart Kids TLC settings, here is the first of three or perhaps four works. Thank you for your constant requests.

Special thanks to the particular individuals who helped uniquely shape this volume—first and foremost my children who had to have the best of everything, including instruction. From infancy through grade school, they were my educational lab kids who ultimately taught me about individual differences among offspring: what one absorbs, the others reject! In their adult years, each has thanked me for being "strong," when all the while I was terrified. Over the years, they have blessed me with seven beautiful, intelligent, and quick-witted grandchildren who now spur me on.

A longtime friend, Betty Moseley-Perry, was among my first clients when Smart Kids, Inc., opened a school. Betty and four other parents drove their children every day from Durham, North Carolina, to Greensboro, approximately fifty-four miles one way. About two years ago, Betty called to ask me to write a book or curriculum for her grandchild. Betty, here is the first in a series of works designed to help parents and grandparents get that peace of mind that comes when they know their children's academic needs are being met. The curriculum is in the pipeline.

Carl (Lut) Williams, my husband, is a syndicated sportswriter. While reading the first draft of this book, he made a facial expression that told me it was not easy to read. I thank him for his most important critique: get to the point!

My dad, Rhody A. McCoy Jr., not only critiqued but also encouraged me during my first year of teaching to make the parents of my students my partners in the education of their children. His recommendation, difficult at first to implement, became invaluable and the cornerstone of my teaching successes.

Arthea B. Perry, whom I have known for decades, knew I was struggling with a format and brought to my house a young man, Daryl Spruiell, who suggested listing twenty-five things parents could do. Identifying twenty-five seemed impossible until I reviewed the files and my recollection of past clients. There were so many recommendations and so much advice covering such a range of topics—including parenting and college preparation—that they had to be divided into categories. His suggestion made the writing task easier. Thank you, both.

Very, very special thanks to the iUniverse staff assigned to me. The editorial staff made comments and critiques that forced me to rethink, rework, and rewrite statements, paragraphs, and sections. This work is a thousand times better because of their comments. Kathi Wittkamper, the editorial consultant, e-mailed dozens of encouraging messages to help me navigate the process and understand that "life happens." Dianne Lee, the check-in coordinator, has also been extremely helpful in making this project a reality.

To all the parents, students, staff members, and supporters who so often held their breath, bit their nails, and hoped and prayed that the advice I gave them would work—thank you for your support, your encouragement, and, most of all, your trust.

Thank God the advice worked most of the time!

INTRODUCTION

Regardless of income, social status, or ethnicity, parents everywhere are concerned about their children's academic performance. We all want our children to reach their academic potential. We all seek the peace of mind that comes with knowing our children are learning and mastering all the skills necessary for academic competence.

Smart Kids TLC (SKTLC) is a tutoring and learning center located in Greensboro, North Carolina. Before teaching or tutoring takes place, children undergo an assessment, primarily in language arts and math, to determine the extent of their needs. In the parental interview, also a part of the assessment, parents are asked by the assessment administrator how SKTLC can help them, the parents. The most frequent answer is "Give me peace of mind." Nothing except their children's health seems more important to them than academic success.

For more than two decades, SKTLC has been providing customized support services to the parents of children in public, private, and charter schools as well as those who are homeschooled. Communication about a child's tutoring progress is frequent, and advice is given to help parents manage their children's learning at home. However, the peace of mind these parents so desperately seek does not come until the child's academic performance stabilizes.

This book and others to follow share some of SKTLC's recommendations and strategies that parents can use to improve their children's academic performance. These can be mixed, matched, and modified to fit specific circumstances, and they have been used by individuals from diverse ethnicities, cultures, socioeconomic strata, and family structures.

Many of the recommendations and strategies are based on research in education, pedagogy, medicine, nutrition, and cognition. Some are traditional and others are nontraditional. Some activities cost money and some don't; however, we always try to suggest inexpensive or free alternatives. At times, the activities will seem unrelated to academics, but each directly or indirectly helps develop intellectual and/or academic abilities. The intention is to provide a range of options from which parents can select to create a holistic and focused plan of action to improve their child's academic experience and performance. No parent can attend to every one of these suggestions, but even one experience will open up a child's mind to new possibilities, which will inevitably improve your children's education and enrich your relationship.

This work is based on three assumptions:

1. Parents deeply care for their children and their children's education even when they do not attend parent-teacher conferences, PTA meetings, or graduations. There are many economic, cultural, and social reasons why parents are invisible in our schools. However, experience tells us that if these parents know the educator is sincerely concerned about their child, they become visible.

2. Parents work and do not have much spare time. Nevertheless, we expect parents to be parents, and we expect them to be proactive. The suggestions—designed to increase the usefulness of your precious moments with your children— may be put into action while doing dishes, cooking, cleaning, driving, traveling, preparing school lunches, getting ready for bed, sitting in waiting rooms, standing in checkout lines, doing laundry, and so on.

3. Parents who cannot read this book will seek help from a family member or close friend who knows about the literacy issue and is willing to assist by reading or explaining. The basis of this assumption is an incident that occurred after I addressed the North Carolina legislature on charter schools. A legislator asked for my thoughts on homeschooling. My response was that illiterate parents could not homeschool. A woman emerged from the crowd to tell me she was illiterate when she decided that, as she put it, "Over my dead body would I ever send my boys to a public school!" Her solution was to ask a friend to help her develop, write, and memorize lesson plans she would then teach to her sons the next day. In the process, she learned to read. She then informed me she was running a school. Where there's a will, there's a way.

Solely for the sake of simplicity and avoidance of pronoun confusion, the parent, teacher and principal are referred to as femaleand the child or student as male. In doing so, no disrespect is intended to any fathers reading this book, male teachers helping students learn, or female students struggling to do their best.

Lastly, despite every attempt to provide accurate and timely information, new research findings may render some information obsolete or in need of modification. What you will read here is the best of my knowledge and research at the time of writing. I hope it will help you begin to achieve the peace of mind you so desperately seek.

Chapter 1

DEVELOPING AN APPROPRIATE MIND-SET

This section is designed to help you lay the foundation for a healthy academic relationship with your child. You will be inspired to take a positive and proactive view of your responsibilities as a parent with respect to your child acquiring a good education.

Today's educational landscape offers options to parents with different perceptions of a good education. Magnet schools and charter schools, for example, draw parents and children who have particular interests, including international education; science and technology; the visual and performing arts; medicine; and foreign languages. Charter schools are both privately and publicly owned, while magnet schools are public schools and therefore technically "owned" by taxpayers.

Parents who view education as the means to a good job may gravitate toward a traditional school, a vocational magnet, or a math-science magnet. Some parents see education as a way to improve one's quality of life, and they may prefer a school that stresses community service, health, or peace. Other parents may feel education should foster creativity and innovation, and so they enroll their children in a school emphasizing the arts. At the opposite end of the spectrum is open or progressive education, which allows children to determine their own pace of learning and make many if not all educational

1

decisions—including what and when to learn. This is also said to foster thought and creativity.

Another model views education as an equalizer—something that encourages and enables children to explore, discover, and work cooperatively toward solutions to issues like environmental pollution and destruction. Some view such schools as liberal, although they are related to John Dewey's theory that the best learning of democracy occurs through practicing democracy. For some ideas about liberal educational goals, albeit at the collegiate level, visit the websites of the National Institute for Technology in Liberal Education at http://www.nitle.org and LEEP (Liberal Education and Effective Practice) at http://www.clarku.edu/leep/ (see http://www.clarku.edu/leep/pioneers2012.cfm for a listing of "2012 LEEP Pioneers and Their Projects").

Also in the mix are the models of Maria Montessori and Jean Piaget. Montessori may have been the very first researcher/practitioner to publicly recognize and discuss children's intelligence or their ability to think, regardless of their social class. Before the industrial era, children of the more financially privileged were thought to have a monopoly on thinking. Variations of the Montessori program continue in the United States. Montessori introduced the scientific approach to the study of intelligence,[1] and Jean Piaget is credited with offering a theory of intellectual development that is gradual and dependent upon a child's physical engagement with his environment. According to Piaget's findings, children are able to think formally (or like adults) between the ages of eleven and fourteen. Piaget's and Montessori's contributions suggest that we can improve education by developing a less teacher-centered curriculum and encouraging more child-centered instruction.[2]

A work-study model dating back to the late 1800s and early 1900s is the cooperative education model, which allows students to work with compensation for one or more semesters or quarters, applying the skills, knowledge, and theories learned in the classroom the previous semester. Cooperative education can give students their first exposure to their intended professional environment. One study suggested cooperative education accelerates a student's learning of "the organizational culture and structure."[3]

The newest educational models are online and increasingly popular with public and private schools. Hundreds of K–12 independent schools are completely online. Regardless of the type of school your child attends, it is our position that—because of the continuous technological advancements in the world of work—all children must receive highly competent instruction in literacy, mathematics, and technology. Unfortunately, too many schools fall short in one or more of these areas, jeopardizing the future and quality of life of thousands of children.

In addition to keeping up with the almost yearly changes in their children's curriculum, parents must vie for their children's attention with such strong forces as after-school activities, influential peers, helpful relatives, and of course electronic devices. On top of these and other social and economic pressures come their youngsters' individual demands for academic attention. Parents need help navigating the sometimes unfamiliar, murky, and changing educational waters while maintaining their sanity. The following suggestions are intended to help you take on the challenge with a good mental attitude.

1. Recognize that all children in the United States are at risk.

Stop assuming that your child is the only one experiencing difficulty. All students in the United States are at risk. Historically, US public schools have produced workers for the industrial sweatshops and farm fields—workers who used their hands, arms, and backs rather than their minds to earn a living. Public schools did not and still do not mass-produce cerebral thinkers or creative workers.

To remain competitive, US businesses in the now well-known STEM fields (science, technology, engineering, and mathematics) have been forced to import workers from other countries who have these skills.[4] High school and college graduates unable to compete for the shrinking number of traditional jobs are demanding the return of the manufacturing base. However, manufacturing has become highly technical and computerized, thus offering far fewer employment opportunities. All our children need high levels of literacy, math, science, and technology to be able to fill the thousands of positions in emerging industries like outer space and renewable energy.

High school dropout rates prior to the 1930s were much higher than today's because the factory and farm provided an abundance of job opportunities. It was not until 1959–1960 that there was an appreciable increase in the high school graduation rate—to 69.5 percent.[5] During WWI (1914–1918), WWII (1939–1945), the Korean War (1950–1953), and the Vietnam War (1955–1975), dropout rates were high but gradually dropped. Graduation rates would not increase until 1969.[6] It could be argued that today's schools are doing exactly what they were designed to do in the early and mid-1900s: minimally educate the masses. Historically, a higher level of education was reserved mostly for rich males. Socialization, the industrial era's overarching goal, remains the goal of today's education—not, as parents might wish, academic achievement or intellectual development.[7]

As of 2008, there were more than nineteen million scientists and mathematicians employed in the United States,[8] and according to businesses, the nation will continue to need more and more STEM specialists. Reasons include the following:

- health care, a growing need for the entire population, young and old
- the environment, including climate change / global warming, pollution, water shortages, topsoil loss, rising oceans, land losses related to the rising oceans, aging infrastructures (roads, buildings, tunnels, bridges, vehicles), and civil and regional conflicts

- renewable energy, outer space, and ocean research—the newer frontiers
- nanotechnology and nanoscience—the miniaturization and computerization of technology

Each area needs youthful and creative minds to solve problems and resolve issues, and our young people are going to need those high-paying jobs: demographic trends (for example, the aging population) suggest that economic burdens like tax, trade, and commerce will fall disproportionately on their shoulders.

Every child, regardless of the circumstances of birth, is extremely valuable. Unfortunately, the politics of education inhibit the production of the type of graduate needed. Administrators and policy makers are caught up in revamping, remodeling, and restructuring schools and programs based on the industrial notion that very few children are smart and the majority are average in intelligence. Curriculum and instruction for the most part continue to be targeted to the average child, which disallows the development of a creative, innovative national mind-set. It falls to parents to promote the view that their children are capable of succeeding in literacy, math, science, and technology.

2. Expect your child to succeed in school.

Many clients confide that they have been told their children are unable to achieve or need a watered-down curriculum to match a slow rate of learning. Too often parents believe what they have been told, especially when confronted with standardized test data and teacher evaluations.

When we analyze our SKTLC assessments of these children, we often discover a lack of basic skills, usually in reading and math. Once the skill deficiencies have been eliminated, the child is usually on the way to achieving success. Moreover, the emergence of the deficiencies frequently corresponds with high teacher absenteeism.

If your child has had one or more teachers who have been repeatedly absent, look for gaps in basic skills before agreeing to labels, retention, or medication. Do not accept that your child should simply be able to catch up. In our experience, children subjected to teacher absences or turnovers rarely independently recover from such educational assaults.

Instead of accepting the teacher's assessment, verbalize to your child your expectations for improvement. Tell your child that each semester, you expect a better performance than the previous semester. Words of encouragement must be frequent and can be expressed in a variety of ways:

- Outright
  - "This grade does not reflect your intelligence."
  - "You can do better than this."
  - "This grade cannot possibly represent your best effort!"
  - "This grade means you did not learn very much. What do you think keeps you from doing better? What are your plans to correct the problem?"
  - "Last semester, you earned a B– average. Do you think you can increase your grade in at least two courses? What will you do differently to achieve the new goal?"
  - "Let's see what happens to your overall average if you increase your letter grade in one course."

- Subtle
  - "Every day, write in your notebook for each course at least one thing you learned so you can share it with the family. Please do not tell us you did not learn anything, because I will have to call your teacher to find out what you missed. If she says she did not teach anything, then I will have to call the principal." (Children in primary school usually do not want their teachers to get into

trouble. Older children need different consequences, because many couldn't care less about their teacher.)

- o "I thought you were proud to be a [last name]. Come on, you're expected to bring admiration to the family / carry on the family tradition!"
- o "Oh, my! What is Grandpa going to say when he sees these grades?"

- Ineffective
  - o "Give your studies the same amount of effort/energy you put into practicing jump shots."

Studies on teacher expectations strongly suggest that teachers who expect success get success, and teachers who expect failure get failure.[9] Similarly, when parents expect success and do not witness it, their words and actions are directed at getting the desired improvements. Parents who expect success create a family culture and climate to support the achievement of success. Most children strive to succeed when they know their parents expect them to be successful.

A comparative study between Asian American children and their mothers and European American children and their mothers was conducted to determine the influence of parenting on student achievement. Findings were that both families wanted their children to succeed; they simply had different ways of promoting that. Asian American mothers hovered over their children while the European American mothers were relaxed and laid back. Parenting styles were not found to be determinants of success. A significant commonality turned out to be high expectations of success.[10]

3. Create a proactive rather than a reactive environment.

Being proactive involves seeing what's coming and planning for that eventuality. If you wait to find out your child's academic status until the report card arrives, it may be too late to change the direction the grades are going. A more proactive approach would be to ask the teacher for a copy of the topics that will be introduced as well as a sample test you can pattern. Assign your child the topics to read *before* instruction, and administer your own tests and quizzes patterned after the teacher's. Information can come from your child's textbook, a library book, a used textbook, the web, or a workbook.

Librarians generally discard old, worn, or unused holdings. Ask your librarian when she will do this so that you can retrieve books, magazines, and pamphlets that relate to the topics your child will be studying. A state university librarian told me she was required to put the literature in the dumpster. As she dropped those books in, I took them out and put them in the trunk of my car.

Ask the teacher for a weekly report of all test, quiz, and homework scores as well as copies of the assessments. To alleviate stress on the teacher, make your child responsible for getting the report from her and bringing it home. After receiving the evidence, examine it and discuss with your child any strengths, weaknesses, and items that need to be addressed. Definitely make your child find out the correct answers, and monitor other activities you assign, such as writing sentences using newly-learned terms.

Being proactive requires that you maintain commitment, consistency, and composure when coaching, tutoring, and teaching. Commitment means you will not give up on your child's learning. Your child undoubtedly has a variety of tactics he uses to get his own way, and in so doing he may get on your last nerve. If you find yourself becoming frustrated or wanting to give up, take a break, count to one thousand if necessary, and then return with a different attitude, tone, approach, or explanation. Remind yourself why you decided to help your child. Your commitment will prove to your reluctant child that he can learn.

Consistency means you deliver on your promises every time. One example is setting aside a specific time during which you and your child will review homework assignments. If you say you will tutor your child in math for an hour each Saturday, do it. If you say you are going to take him to the museum, take him. If you state that he must complete his assignment before going outside, make sure he has done it before he goes.

Classic examples of inconsistency are parental threats of "If you do this one more time, I will …" or "I'll give you one more chance." Instead, apply consequences previously established by both of you. Your child will continue to love you unconditionally even when you scold or discipline. Do not be part of the problem.

Remain calm regardless of what your child says or does. Some parents become unglued when their child resists help, fails to understand, or cries and whines. Explore the reasons for the resistance. Perhaps your child thinks peers or teachers will say something negative when they find out he is being helped. Address these fears. Describe or demonstrate an appropriate reaction if and when peers do find out. Your child may have an undying faith in teachers or peers and refuse to believe anything different from what they have said. In these instances, it is usually best to be positive about the teacher or peers. Gently insist that you can also help because there are different ways to tackle problems, including schoolwork.

Your message, body language, and facial expressions must match. When your child objects, whines, cries, pouts, or has a temper tantrum, use body language consistent with your tone and words—together, they must send a clear, consistent, and composed message. Speak firmly without smiling and without raising your voice. An example of body language conveying a message of no nonsense is simply moving closer while speaking to your child, which to a child is intimidating.

When you feel your blood beginning to boil or your patience waning, take a fifteen- to twenty-minute break to collect your thoughts. Remember this: when you yell, your child has gained control. If you lose your composure, apologize and tell your child you will try not to lose your temper again—and really work on it. Instead of anger and confrontation, use your parent powers to get your child to cooperate: the power of the purse, the power to take away what has been given, the power to deny what has been requested, and the power to levy consequences. These are much more effective.

Sometimes parents lose composure when their children accept help but repeatedly say "I don't get it" or "I don't understand." A parent who is frustrated when a child does not do or understand the work often ends up giving too much help, and so the phrase may be the child's way of getting the parent to cancel the session or take over. If your child lights up when you offer help or gets up to leave you to do his homework, you may have already established a pattern of giving in. When you do the work, you're the one who is learning, not your child. Furthermore, your child is no longer taking responsibility for his education.

Think about and write down how your child has managed to get you to help. Study and resist these methods of persuasion. Remember your goal should be to get your child to help himself and take responsibility for his studies.

4. Emphasize learning rather than high grades.

Higher grades do not necessarily mean a better grasp of information. The ability to apply knowledge is a better measure of learning. To help your child learn how to apply information, ask why it is important and when and how it can be used. Then ask for a minimum of three uses of the information. If your child has difficulty coming up with answers, do not panic; rather, remember that children have limited experiences. Suggest looking in textbooks, because answers to these questions are usually stated (some may be in the back of the book in an answers section). Tell your child to go beyond the textbook's information to demonstrate understanding and ability to apply the concepts. Ask for applications similar to those in the texts.

Learning can also be enhanced and emphasized while developing the healthy habit of drinking water. Tell your child that drinking a glass of water before doing homework increases his ability to learn. Studies have shown that learning, thought, concentration, alertness, visual attention, and performance on tests can be improved by drinking water, which provides the oxygen needed for the brain's proper functioning. Serve water to give your child an intellectual boost.[11]

5. Vary the time to learn concepts from child to child and subject to subject.

Teachers and administrators often refer to "individual differences," yet the rate of instruction is usually inflexible. If your child complains he does not understand, he may be falling behind. If your child complains he is bored, he may not understand what is being said or taught, or perhaps he is not being challenged. Tutoring is reasonable, may be offered by the school, and should be explored; however, consider supplementing learning with activities related to the topics being taught and those with which your child is having difficulty. Children need enrichment when they're not challenged.

Libraries often have materials on different topics at different reading levels, from the primary grades through high school. Librarians can identify books on the topic and level you are seeking. If the library does not have a copy of a book you desire, ask about an interlibrary loan or adding the book to the library's collection. The latter may take a while.

Teachers do not have the time or resources to use each and every child's strengths and interests to explain a concept, but you may be able to do that for your child. Start by asking yourself the following questions:

- Does he express himself well? If he does, ask him to explain the concept, give examples to you, and then write in his notebook the responses he just gave.

- Does he have good writing skills? If he does, have him neatly write explanations and examples to use as notes or reminders of details he may otherwise forget.
- Does he have good listening skills or a good listening memory? If so, read or tell him the concept and then ask him to develop a memory device (mnemonic) to help *you* recall the information with ease. As he teaches you the mnemonic, he practices and applies what he knows.

Your child's interests may also be used to strengthen a concept of the topic:

- If he likes to draw, have him draw a scene to illustrate his understanding.
- If he likes animals, art, sports, or machines, ask him to come up with examples of the concept in animal behavior or sports or machine operations.
- If he loves to tell stories, encourage him to create a story using information he is learning; perhaps it can be recorded on video.
- If he likes to write, have him write a story or a poem to demonstrate comprehension and ability to apply the concepts.

6. Prepare for frequent and varied practice opportunities.

Children learn and master concepts and skills through repetition, periodic review, additional reading, and concept manipulation using games, demonstrations, construction, experiments, plays, poems, and so forth. Through repeating the same or similar activities, your child becomes more and more familiar with the concept. The more he knows about a topic, the more he recalls and applies.

Workbooks in literacy, mathematics, social sciences, and science are readily available in stores like Dollar Tree, Walmart, and Target.

Look for workbooks with explanations, examples, and illustrations to help with the explanation. Each workbook should be from the same company for a smooth transition from one grade level to the next and for continuity in concept development. To build confidence and enjoyment from the extra work, start with workbooks two grades below your child's so as to ensure the opportunity to correctly answer most if not all of the questions. Workbooks also allow your child to identify and develop skills that may have been missed along the way.

Each night have your child complete a total number of pages equivalent to his age. A twelve-year-old completes a total of twelve pages a night, for example. If answers are in the back of the book, allow your child to check his answers after finishing problems on the page or in the section. Explain that the answers are available for checking work and applying what has been learned and that using the answers improperly only hurts him. If your child repeatedly copies the answers, remove the answers.

Although many schools have websites with supplemental information and exercises for both students and parents, your child may require additional practice, explanations, and/or examples. Search the web for sites that offer how-to directions and practice activities. You can also ask his teacher to help by reviewing the process or procedure with your child. Try not to make such requests too often.

If your child is old enough, consider allowing him to google websites that offer help in his areas of weakness. For example, he can google "free online punctuation exercises" to see what pops up. No access to a computer? The local library should have computers with Internet access, and you can ask your child's teacher or school librarian if she would allow some free time during which children may research topics of their own choice. If she does, be sure to ask your child to show you what he accessed.

7. Be aware that state standards identify the *least* a child must know.

A state's competencies are the least amount of knowledge, concepts, and skills your child is expected to learn and know. Therefore, what is taught and what happens in the classroom should cover more than what is required by the Every Student Succeeds Act, Common Core standards, and each state's standards and competencies. Unfortunately, standards and competencies are often viewed as goals of instruction. To combat this flawed thinking, parents should—to the best of their ability and regardless of the neighborhood, ethnicity, or income— enrich or supplement their children's learning. The local library should have computers with Internet access if you don't have access at home. Expose your child to visual and performing arts, foreign languages, physical education, shop, and vocational education courses. See also chapter 4 on developing a repertoire of experiences.

Another important point that many parents overlook, especially parents of elementary and middle school children, is requirements for admission to the state university system. Please do not wait until your child is in the ninth grade to look at the course requirements, especially if your child is college bound. SKTLC recommends to parents that their children have four years each of English, literature, a foreign language, mathematics, and physical education; three years each of science and history and/or geography and/or government and/or civics; and one year each of US history and personal finance / consumer literacy.

8. Establish ground rules for the school year *before* school starts.

Ground rules actually set the educational climate and parental tone for academic learning throughout the household. You are conveying the notion that academic achievement is serious business:

good grades result in economic success. When community colleges are free of charge, a not-so-obvious result will be fierce competition for the few seats available. When manufacturing jobs come back, there will be a demand for highly skilled graduates of community colleges.[12]

Ground rules should definitely include your expectations for the following:

- in-school and out-of-school behavior
- telephone and electronic use, not only on school nights but also on weekends
- socialization with friends
- daily and weekly chores
- homework/study schedule
- organization of school materials and supplies, including book bag with appropriate notebooks, pencils, rulers, compass
- lunch / lunch money
- school transportation

When you make a threat or establish a consequence, you *must* follow through. Do not threaten to kill, maim, or break; your child knows you cannot or will not do so. Failure to follow through makes a child think your threats are meaningless and therefore you are not serious when you make them.

If establishing ground rules is new to the family, expect your child to test your consistency. Some children ask the same question over and over again until the mother gives in. Generally, the mother has given in to this type of demand before—you only have to give in once to set up this bad habit. Teach very early in life that no means no and that asking more than twice treads on your respect, feelings, rights, and composure.

Ground rules may also address children's expectations of themselves and family members. Ask your children what they expect for themselves and their siblings. For instance, a ten-year-old may state that he wants to do homework without being asked. You may offer to give an incentive after four or five consecutive times he does assignments without being asked. Another child may make a reasonable request for his sister to stop teasing or calling him names when he does not get a good grade. Levy a consequence on the sister each time, especially the first time she teases or calls names. A practical ground rule is that siblings should help each other with their studies instead of attacking and tearing each other apart. Sibling support may have to be monitored to ensure one child does not use the other to do his homework.

As your child reaches middle school, consider making a ground rule that phones, social media, and electronic devices must be checked by you and taken out of reach when not being used for educational purposes. You may be surprised to find that during class time or homework sessions, your child has been spending valuable minutes chatting with others. Some children become involved in ways that parents would never imagine—visit the listing of US Sexting Laws on the Mobile Media Guard site at http://mobilemediaguard.com/state_main.html to learn more about one type of trouble your child could get into. All states have these laws on their books.

Some parents feel they should do the checking with their child present or with their child's permission. Whatever you choose to do, remember a child has no right to privacy, and in some instances you, as purchaser of the device, may be held criminally and civilly liable for laws broken by your child. In most states, there is no age limit.

9. Encourage your child to value education.

Although education may be a family priority, children need to realize the struggles individuals have undergone to improve their own and their family's lot through education. For ethnic minorities and the poor, education has historically been one of the few roads to success, dignity, and economic advancement. Today, education is rapidly becoming an important economic factor for everyone. Yet at the very time doors of opportunity are swinging wide open for those skilled in communications, technology, mathematics, and science, too many children are failing to value a quality education. You may wish to consider doing a few of the following:

Repeat frequently to your child that a quality education must be his goal, regardless of what his peers think, say, or do.

Have your child interview relatives about their struggles with learning while taking notes and/or recording the interview.

Model for your children the importance of learning by letting them see you read and discussing with others factual information many children find boring.

Conduct a family film festival with three to five movies showing people struggling for a better life for others and for themselves. Preview each to determine its appropriateness for children. Develop discussion points, such as the historical events of the times depicted that allowed the social conditions to flourish. Good choices to consider include *The Diary of Anne Frank* (1959), *Roll of Thunder, Hear My Cry* (1978), *The Life and Times of Rosie the Riveter* (1980), *Gandhi* (1982), *Mississippi Burning* (1988), *The Attic: The Hiding of Anne Frank* (1988), *Glory* (1989), *Searching for Bobby Fischer* (1993), *Erin Brockovich* (2000), *Something the Lord Made* (2004), *Bury My Heart at Wounded Knee* (2007), *American Revolutionary: The Evolution of Grace Lee Boggs* (2013), and for mature older children, *Dark Matter* (2008).

Talk about the battles waged well before and after the 1954 *Brown v. Board of Education of Topeka* court case. Occasionally recite for your children some of the sacrifices their parents, grandparents, and great grandparents made so that they could get a decent education. (Don't overdo it!)

10. Help your child make academic studies his number one priority.

How a child spends time after school and over the weekend may reflect whether academics are in fact the family's number one priority. Examine how you and your children spend time and money on, for example, entertainment. Are there more educational or noneducational toys, games, books, television programming, and vacations being consumed? Compare after-school time spent on academic and nonacademic activities to determine which takes up the most time. Organizational and hygienic tasks like making one's bed and emptying the trash do not take much time and should not be a part of the activities being examined. However, if a child cannot complete both chores and homework by a reasonable bedtime, consider moving chores to the weekend.

Bedtime also reflects whether academics are a family priority. Children need their rest, and several studies have found teenagers in particular do not get adequate hours of sleep, yet they are more likely to stay up well beyond ten at night.[13] Teachers complain about teens falling asleep in class. In fairness, the homework load may require children to stay up late. If this and extracurricular activities are a problem, consider asking the president of the parent-teacher association to discuss the issue in one or more meetings so that recommendations may be made to the administration, teachers, and parents.

A teen working twenty hours or less during the school week may or may not challenge the family's emphasis on education. There are studies suggesting teens who work less than twenty hours during the school week are better at using their free time to study. However, in 2011, several collaborating universities issued a report stating that allowing teens to work more than twenty hours a week opens the door to unforeseen consequences related to lack of sleep, including behavioral and academic difficulties, dropping out, vehicular deaths, workplace injuries, and violence.[14] If your child works, ask each of his teachers whether he falls asleep in class. If he does, then ensure that he gets to bed by eleven and rises at a reasonable time. An alternative is to have your child ask his supervisor whether work hours can be reduced or distributed over the weekend.

Sometimes a sleepy student is working to support a family. If possible, parents should help out so that education, financial support, and adequate sleep are all provided for. Once again, try your best to get your children to bed at a regular time each school night, including Sunday.

Notes

1   "Maria Montessori Biography," Biography.com, accessed April 26, 2015, http://www.biography.com/people/maria-montessori-9412528.

2   J. Roy Hopkins, "The Enduring Influence of Jean Piaget," *Observer* 24, no. 10 (December 2011), http://www.psychologicalscience.org/index.php/publications/observer/2011/december-11/jean-piaget.html; "Jean Piaget," NNDB, accessed April 26, 2015, http://www.nndb.com/people/359/000094077/.

3   Patricia L. Linn, Adam Howard, and Eric Miller, *Handbook for Research in Cooperative Education and Internships* (Mahwah, NJ: Lawrence Erlbaum Associates, 2004): 377, 379; *History of Agricultural Education of Less than College Grade in the United States: A Cooperative Project of Workers in Vocational Education in Agriculture and in Related Fields,* compiled by Rufus W. Stimson and Frank W. Lathrop (Washington: US Government Printing Office, 1942).

4   Linda Rosen, "The Truth Hurts: The STEM Crisis Is Not a Myth," *Huffington Post*, September 11, 2013, http://www.huffingtonpost.com/linda-rosen/the-truth-hurts-the-stem-_b_3900575.html; Parija Kavilanz, "American Manufacturers Importing Workers," CNN Money, July 23, 2012, http://money.cnn.com/2012/03/05/smallbusiness/manufacturing-workers/.

5   "High School Graduates, by Sex and Control of School: Selected Years, 1869–70 through 2019–20," National Center for Education Statistics, accessed April 26, 2015, http://nces.ed.gov/programs/digest/d10/tables/dt10_110.asp

6   Christopher B. Swanson, June 2, 2010, "Graduation Rate Continues Decline," Education Week, http://www.edweek.org/ew/articles//210/06/10/34swanson. H29.html

7   "Colonial Education," Stratford Hall, accessed April 26, 2015, http://www.stratfordhall.org/educational-resources/teacher-resources/colonial-education/; Eleanor Putnam, "A Salem Dame School," *The Atlantic Monthly* 55, no. 327 (January 1885), http://ebooks.library.cornell.edu/cgi/t/text/pageviewer-idx?c=atla;cc=atla;rgn=full%20text;idno=atla0055-1;didno=atla0055-1;view=image;seq=0059;node=atla0055-1%3A8.

8   Michael Teitelbaum, "The Myth of the Science and Engineering Shortage," *The Atlantic*, March 19, 2014,

http://www.theatlantic.com/education/archive/2014/03/
the-myth-of-the-science-and-engineering-shortage/284359/.

9   Alix Spiegel, "Teachers' Expectations Can Influence How Students
Perform," *Shots*, NPR, *Morning Edition*, September 17, 2012, http://www.
npr.org/blogs/health/2012/09/18/161159263/teachers-expectations-
can-influence-how-students-perform.

10 Ruth K. Chao, "Chinese and European American Mothers' Beliefs about
the Role of Parenting in Children's School Success," *Journal of Cross-
Cultural Psychology* 27, no. 4 (July 1996): 403–423, http://jcc.sagepub.
com/content/27/4/403.abstract.

11 Barry Popkin, Kristen D'Anci, and Irwin Rosenberg, "Water, Hydration,
and Health," *Nutrition Reviews* 68, no. 8 (2010): 439–458, http://www.
ncbi.nlm.nih.gov/pmc/articles/PMC2908954/; Anisha Patel and Karla
Hampton, "Encouraging Consumption of Water in School and Child
Care Settings: Access, Challenges, and Strategies for Improvement,"
American Journal of Public Health 101, no. 8 (August 2011): 1370–1379,
http://www.ncbi.nlm.nih.gov/pmc/articles/PMC3134515/; D. Benton
and N. Burgess, "The Effect of Consumption of Water on the Memory
and Attention of Children," *Appetite* 53, no.1 (August 2009), 143–6,
http://www.ncbi.nlm.nih.gov/pubmed/19445987.

12 Parija Kavilanz, "American Manufacturers Importing Workers,"
July 23, 2012, http://money.cnn.com/2012/03/05/smallbusiness/
manufacturing-workers/.

13 "Teens and Sleep," National Sleep Foundation, accessed April 26, 2015,
http://sleepfoundation.org/sleep-topics/teens-and-sleep.

14 NCL Staff, "Working More than 20 Hours a Week Is a Bad Idea for
Teens," National Consumers League, April 2011, http://www.nclnet.org/
working_more_than_20_hours_a_week_is_a_bad_idea_for_teens.

Chapter 2

ESTABLISHING EDUCATIONAL GOALS AND OBJECTIVES

Goals give meaning, purpose, and direction to your child's educational pursuits. They also help reduce procrastination—every student's enemy—as well as save time and energy. Goals are broad and lofty, usually reflecting a dream or hope, and should be clearly written and periodically reviewed to help your child focus and refocus attention on the reasons, purposes, importance, and direction of his education. Goals also take time to accomplish, from a month to a semester, term, or number of years.

Objectives are steps toward a goal. They are specific, detailed, and more often than not action oriented. Just as a goal may have several objectives, an objective may entail many activities that physically and emotionally engage your child to meet the objectives' requirements.

11. Establish educational goals, objectives, and activities for all family members.

Educational goals state the family's desired outcome for the children. For example, "Each child will attend either a two-year or a four-year college." Children have a stake in learning and should be involved in the establishment of educational goals. Embedded in the goal is a belief about the purpose of education, which when clarified results in lofty but more specific goals, such as the following:

- If you believe education prepares children for the workforce or paves the way to a good-paying job or position, a family goal may be that each child will meet the requirements to enter and graduate from a vocational or four-year college.
- If you believe education prepares a child to immediately enter the workforce after graduation, the goal may be that each child will find employment after graduation.
- If you believe higher education produces leaders, a goal may be that each child will aspire to become a leader in a particular field.
- If you believe education improves the quality of life or makes one a better person or world citizen, the goal may be that each child will attend and graduate from a liberal arts college or major in the humanities, such as literature or philosophy.

Of course, goals can also reflect a belief that education has more than one purpose. For example, if you think education improves the quality of life and prepares one for the workforce, an appropriate educational goal may be employment in a field projected to yield an income that allows a standard of living higher than that of parents and grandparents.

Objectives give direction and help clarify the steps needed to attain a goal. Two objectives may be to complete all homework assignments every night and to read an extra book each month. For the college-bound child, an objective may be to identify the courses necessary for attending state universities; another is to earn grades of B or higher in those courses. For the work-bound child, an objective may be to research high school courses required by a prospective employer in his field of interest; another objective would be to find out what additional training—such as an apprenticeship—may be needed in addition to high school training.

By the way, there are high-paying jobs that require only a high school diploma. Both the college-bound and non-college-bound should read "40 High-Paying Jobs That Don't Require a Bachelor's Degree" by Vivian Glang (http://jobs.aol.com/articles/2013/12/30/40-high-paying-jobs-that-dont-require-a-bachelors-degree/) and "The Seven Best Paying Jobs with Only a High School Diploma" by Thomas C. Frohlich (http://247wallst.com/special-report/2013/08/26/the-best-paying-jobs-with-a-high-school-diploma/). Remind your child that competition for jobs and seats in a college will always be high, which means grades remain important.

Common to all these approaches to setting goals is the need to know how each system works. Though the goals of students and parents may differ, the process by which to achieve these goals can unite members of different generations. Regardless of intent, parents must help children understand that these choices must not be made lightly—that there are reasons for the way things work.

Some children assume that because teachers review at the beginning of each year, it is unnecessary to retain, practice, and review information or schoolwork previously learned. Understand that children's reasoning has not fully developed; you must bring to their attention the physical impossibility of teachers reviewing within a few weeks or months *everything* covered over the previous nine or ten months. Objectives to help with this common but invalid assumption involve using and applying skills learned in previous years: to write complete sentences, to make an outline before writing a speech or research paper, to practice multiplication tables, and to review twice a week the notes, tests, and quizzes from the year's coursework. This sort of application of lessons learned in previous years is something teachers really like to see.

Activities are what children do to accomplish their objectives. One activity for both college- and workforce-bound students—beginning with their *first year* of high school—is taking courses previously identified as preparatory for college or work. For the objective to develop good written and spoken communication skills, an activity may be joining public speaking and debate clubs or the newspaper and yearbook staff.

Family activities can involve identifying, booking/scheduling, and preparing for the children's or family's weekly, monthly, or yearly activities—an academic quiz bowl with questions and answers taken from notes, textbooks, or quizzes, for example, or a visit to a local science, history, or art museum. Ask your child's teacher to recommend an educational trip or event related to a concept she teaches or may teach in the near future.

12. Verbalize to your child your expectations for each academic semester.

When establishing goals, tell your child you expect increased improvement each semester. Make sure to evaluate long-term objectives and goals so you can communicate what it takes to accomplish them.

Improvement usually takes time, so a demand for great improvement each grading period may be too stressful. Studies on teacher expectations strongly suggest that teachers who expect high levels of performance from their students get high levels of performance, and teachers who expect low levels of performance get low levels of performance.[15]

Caution: you must believe your child is capable of achieving at higher levels. Your belief or disbelief will be expressed through your choice of words, sentences, facial expressions, and actions. Children sense insincerity, so you must believe what you say or refrain from saying anything. Do not express your doubts about your children's abilities in their presence or when they are in the house; you will demoralize them.

Suppose your son earns a 40 on his first math test. You can tell him you expect a five to seven point increase on the next test. Then, when he increases his test or quiz score, praise him. But rather than saying, "See! I told you you could do it!" ask him what he did to bring about the increase. Sometimes a child is aware of the changes he makes and is willing to share them. If he says he doesn't know, suggest some possibilities. Did he complete his homework assignments regularly? Did he study for his test in a different way? Did he simply decide to get a better grade? Inquire whether he thinks it is possible to earn more points if he makes additional changes. Ask what those changes might be, and say that for his next test you are sure he can produce a greater point increase, perhaps five or ten points. Make a deal, for example, if he increases the next test score by 5 points, he may ___ (he fills in the blank with your approval, of course).

This type of discussion empowers your child to take the decision-making responsibility for learning. Moreover, the strategy may help you avoid applying undue stress. When verbalizing your expectations, keep in mind that although your child may have the potential to achieve at higher levels, he may be unable to do so for a variety of reasons. For example, if you ask him why he is not performing better, he may say he dislikes the subject. Yet his dislike for the subject may be related to struggling to understand what he is reading. If he says he is bored, he may be expressing a lack of understanding of what he reads.

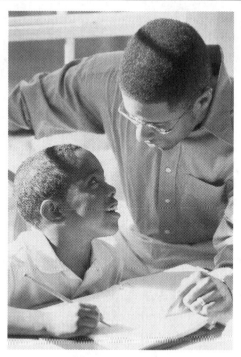

Frequently, the lack of comprehension can be removed simply by improving vocabulary. Before reading the text, having your child scan for and substitute unfamiliar words with familiar synonyms from a dictionary or thesaurus may make comprehension easier. Have your child learn the definition of all unknown words because they will come up again and again—that is a promise.

13. Realize you may have to help your child improve.

A few possible barriers to academic improvement are a lack of the necessary supplies; a lack of adequate parental monitoring of progress; inadequate parental supervision of nonacademic activities (electronic games, telephone usage, the opposite gender); domestic disturbances/problems; social media distractions; and inadequate sleep. For these areas, the cures are obvious—and you, the parent, have some control over these obstacles. Yet some barriers are beyond parental control.

The following suggestions can help you help your child (but understand that some involve asking a teacher to act out of the ordinary):

- Ask his teacher to identify for you the skills he needs to correctly answer missed questions on a test.
- Ask the teacher to text you each time your child comes unprepared and lacking the proper tools needed to learn, such as pencils, pens, compass, ruler, protractor, notebooks, homework, projects, and reports. When you receive such a text, levy a consequence for not having prepared the night before.
- When your child expresses a disinterest in specific topics or courses, on a weekend at the library have him research five to seven interesting things related to the topic or course, but from other fields, such as geography, economics, politics, government, or art. He must also record his sources (a habit you want to develop), including author, title, and volume of the work; page number, date of publication, and ISBN; or author, title, date of publication, website URL, and date accessed. Ask if he would care to share his findings with the teacher and his classmates—after all, education/ knowledge is important for all. If the suggestion is in line with the teacher's objectives, she may say yes. If she denies the request, have him present the information to the family, church, or a group to which he belongs.

That last suggestion works best for younger children. For older children, a different strategy may be needed, such as a brief or formal essay question, poem, song, letter, play, or short story about his findings, which can be given to his teacher to avoid embarrassment. If the list of research topics is unappealing to your child, encourage him to ask the teacher if he may substitute one of his own, similar to his teacher's. What is interesting about offering alternatives is that the child actually does extra work—after researching the topic, he then must think about, plan, and deliver his nontraditional method of presentation.

14. Remind your child that his major responsibility is to become well educated.

The terms *well educated* and *well rounded* are often used interchangeably. However, there is a difference: a well-educated person has successfully completed his education and demonstrates his well-roundedness by deftly utilizing the skills and knowledge acquired. Neither term means the person earned straight As. To many, a well-educated person is well read and able to converse logically and clearly in Standard English on a variety of topics coming from a variety of fields.

Well-roundedness is the opposite of one-sidedness or lopsidedness with respect to the majority of courses pursued. Many liberal arts universities try to ensure a well-rounded graduate by requiring a specific number of credit hours in the humanities (literature, art, philosophy), social sciences (history, economics, geography), and natural sciences (astronomy, physics, chemistry, and biology). The well-rounded and well-educated person has also read a variety of literary works in several genres (novels, poetry, satire, plays) and communicates well in both writing and speaking. Graduates from technical and vocational schools take liberal arts courses to achieve the well-roundedness their employers expect of graduates. Ideally, your child will be well educated, because this assumes well-roundedness.

Activities help you define what you as a parent consider necessary for your child to be well educated. Some believe well rounded means having and showing compassion for the less fortunate; they have their children volunteer in shelters or soup kitchens. Others believe well rounded and well educated mean possessing an appreciation of the arts and thus endure their child learning to play a musical instrument, learning lines in a play, or pursuing ballet. Some put their children in settings related to the child's career aspirations: a photographer's helper, a candy striper, or a computer shop assistant. These positions may or may not be volunteer, and many parents prefer volunteerism so that children realize the fortunate can and should help the less fortunate without pay.

Well-roundedness can be most beneficial. For example, a candidate for admission to a prestigious college walked into an interview that would decide his admission. As he was sitting down, he noticed a painting on the wall and casually commented that he liked that particular style of painting. After he and the admissions officer completed a long and lively discussion on Impressionism, the counselor stood up, extended his hand, and said, "Young man, welcome to the university!" The young man's actual area of interest was business and finance. As an elective in high school he had taken an art course where he discovered his liking for the particular style. It takes years to develop well-rounded, well-educated children; your commitment, consistency, and composure are the keys to achieving your family's educational goals.

Notes

15 Thomas L. Good, "Two Decades of Research on Teacher Expectations: Findings and Future Directions," *Journal of Teacher Education* 38, issue 4 (July 1987): 32–47, http://jte.sagepub.com/content/38/4/32.abstract; Robert Rosenthal and Lenore Jacobson, *Pygmalion in the Classroom: Teacher Expectation and Pupils' Intellectual Development* (Wales, UK: Crown House Publishing, 2013); "The Pygmalian Effect," Center for Teaching Excellence, Dusquene University, accessed April 26, 2015, http://www. duq.edu/about/centers-and-institutes/center-for-teaching-excellence/ teaching-and-learning/pygmalion.

Chapter 3

ASSISTING WITH HOMEWORK AND ASSIGNMENTS

Homework can be a headache for both students and parents. These tips are designed to help reduce tension for both.

15. Find out why homework is assigned.

At the beginning of the school term, when most schools have an open house, ask your child's teacher how she will use homework. The following are some of the possible purposes of homework:

- *Brief review*—homework is assigned at the child's "independent level," which means the child has no need for adult assistance because the work is one or two grade levels below the child's. Most children take twenty or thirty minutes to complete this work, and to parents, the assignments seem too easy. Parents generally dislike assignments like these.

- *Practice and application*—assignments are usually at the independent level but not necessarily below grade level. Often, these assignments have twenty or thirty problems to solve, or two or more essays to write, in addition to textbook questions, especially those requiring time to respond and/or reflect. Some parents dislike these assignments because they consume most of the child's evening, preventing quality time for the family.

- *Classroom extension*—teachers assign mandated material they are unable to cover in class. The teacher either assumes the student has the skills required to fulfill the assignment or the material is at the child's independent level. For example, chapters are assigned, and there are questions in the textbook or from the teacher to be answered. Often, the assignments are discussed in class the next day. Another example is literature that if covered in class would consume too much time. Again, the literature is discussed in class.

- *Enrichment*—assignments are designed to broaden a child's knowledge. Such assignments are less frequent in low-income schools. Although application and practice may be involved, the intent is to deepen the learning experience. The assumption is that the child has the skills (and maybe the money) to complete the task. Sometimes parental involvement is sought or required. For example, a class studying Colonial America might take a trip to historic Williamsburg, Virginia. Projects also provide enrichment.

- *Instructional level*—children need adult instruction, guidance, and/or assistance to satisfactorily complete the assignment. Parents often despise this form of homework because they do not have the skills, the knowledge, or the time to provide that help. There are a variety of reasons a teacher might use homework in this way. Be sure to ask.

16. Make certain your child understands the homework directions.

Struggling readers may be unclear about what is expected of them. After children silently read the homework directions, parents can ask them to explain what they think they are supposed to do. Confusion often comes from not knowing the meaning of the words in the directions. Math word problems especially give children a challenge, frequently for the same reason: vocabulary.

Have your child look up unknown words in the dictionary, define each, and learn the meanings; those words are sure to come up over and over again. For example, an assignment may be to research and write a report on the economic issues surrounding the outbreak of the bubonic plague in the fourteenth century. If your child does not know the meaning of *issue*, then his answer will be incorrect or inadequate. *Issue* is a word that forever will be in his life, so he needs to learn its multiple meanings.

17. Improve recall of concepts in home assignments through questioning.

Children often memorize details because they think it's easier or they do not completely understand the information. To encourage comprehension and retention of information, ask questions about the homework assignment and about in-class lessons that relate to the assignment. Ability to recall the information increases when your child can explain the concept.

Ask questions daily until it becomes something your child expects. Usually children prepare for questions when they know their parents will ask for examples, a demonstration, how the information helps them, or how they would use the concept or skill. Although textbooks usually state the importance or reason for learning the concept and give real-life examples children may be able to relate to, ask your child to think of one or two more real-life examples or applications.

18. Question your child on what he learned in each of his classes.

Ask questions not only about the homework but also about in-class lessons (such as who, what, when, where, why, how; characteristics, steps or stages; history of, reasons for). Ask for an explanation of concepts introduced, learned, reviewed or discussed. Knowing you'll be asking about the lesson, your child may pay closer attention in class or ask the teacher the same questions as preparation for giving you the answers.

19. Regularly check assignments for errors in grammar, content, and completion.

Usually when children know their work will be checked and challenged, they take more care and time doing their assignments. When you ask, "Have you done your homework?" and your child answers yes, follow up by asking him to bring the assignments to you so you can look them over. Look to see if study aids (such as date, book title, and page number) are listed at the top of the page. Dates help locate a particular activity, example, note, or assignment your child may be seeking.

Check to see if the answers are neatly written and in complete sentences; one-word responses are often unacceptable to teachers trying to teach sentence construction. If possible, check to ensure that the answers match the question. Essays should contain supporting details (like facts, descriptions, justifications, explanations), and sources of the information should be identified.

When errors are found, tell your child to make the corrections or find the correct answers by using the appropriate source: a grammar book, the index in the back of the textbook, *Bartlett's Familiar Quotations*, libraryspot.com, or another reliable source.

20. Encourage your child to put information into his own words.

Young children have difficulty understanding plagiarism—the theft of someone's ideas and words. Older children ignore serious consequences, such as expulsion from school, loss of employment, lawsuits, and loss of income. Instead of copying word for word, your child should be rewording an author's printed statement to demonstrate understanding of what has been read or said—this is known as *paraphrasing*—as well as giving credit to the author of the statement.

Even when the author's thoughts and statements have been restated, credit must be given; otherwise, it is plagiarism. Ask your child's English teacher if she would give you pointers on paraphrasing.

Students should always retain a hard copy and/or an electronic copy for their records of any submission to the teacher. Teachers are human and can misplace or spill coffee on a paper. E-mailing a submission to the teacher is a good idea because there is documentation of not only the day but also the time the submission was made.

21. Give your child a movement break when fatigue sets in from doing homework.

Suggest your child take a ten- to fifteen-minute break and do one of the following:

- Change his study location.
- Stretch, do a few push-ups, or shoot five hoops.
- Get a snack.
- Make a sketch or illustration of what he is reading or practicing.
- Take a five- to ten-minute walk.
- Play with his pet for ten minutes.

Chapter 4

BUILDING A REPERTOIRE OF EXPERIENCES

This section suggests relatively inexpensive out-of-school activities that provide experiences to build competencies in mathematics, science, social studies, economics, geography, agriculture, literacy, the arts, and more. Specifically, the activities increase the understanding of concepts taught in school; connect abstract ideas to real people, places, and events; and improve thinking skills (such as drawing conclusions and inferences) that require information beyond the text.

22. Provide educational activities that reinforce topics learned in school.

Fortunately, the average home is filled with learning opportunities related to topics children learn in school:

- Cooking reinforces math, reading, physics, and chemistry.
- Shopping reinforces math, consumerism, and personal finance.
- Family genealogy reinforces history.
- Hygiene reinforces concepts in biology and chemistry.

- Saving money reinforces planning, math (interest, percent), and personal finance.
- Gardening reinforces biology, chemistry, meteorology, and physics.

Ask your child what his interests and concerns are and include them among the activities.

23. Enter your child into academics-related competitions that match his interests.

Competitions educate, excite, and motivate children. They expand experiences that can be applied when reading. Competitions may be local, by county, by state, and regional. The following are sites to explore for competitions or ideas:

- "Photography Contests for Kids" by Stephanie M. Kelley, http://photography.lovetoknow.com/Young_ Photography_Contests
- "Lorian Hemingway Short Story Competition," http:// shortstorycompetition.com/Guidelines.php
- "Eight Writing Contests for Kids" by Amanda Morin, http://kidsactivities.about.com/od/ReadingandWriting/tp/ Writing-Contests-For-Kids.htm
- "National Geographic Bee," http://www.nationalgeo-graphic.com/geobee
- National Spelling Bee, http://spellingbee.com/students -parents

24. Expose your child to a variety of experiences for a broader knowledge base.

Although no definitive number or types of experiences have been identified, state competencies/standards have been used to define the parameters of children's experiences. The difficulty is that the competencies address minimums, so each child is expected to know more.

Below is a tiny sampling of activities that provide experiences useful in reading, writing, thinking, exemplifying, or ideating in literature, science, social studies, economics, geography, history, and other subjects. Before investing money, first investigate the web's offerings, such as museums and art galleries. Many of the following can be found online for free.

- *Sites to visit*—call to find out the schedule of events and fees, if any, for the following:

art museums	art galleries	maritime museums
clock museums	plantations	planetariums
universities	stock exchanges	brokerage houses
banks	aquariums	zoological parks
gardens	ethnic museums/galleries	
parks (local and national)		mountains
beaches	deserts	plains
forests	farms	fisheries
orchards	post offices	United Nations
courthouses	governmental offices	
firehouses	police stations	factories
doctor's offices	dentist's offices	shipyards
architect's offices	artist's studios	marinas
carpenter's workshops		airfields
web designer's studios		supermarkets
mechanic's garages	film studios	research parks
libraries (special, research, Congressional)		castles
ships	submarines	battlefields
historical monuments, buildings, cities, and cemeteries		

- *Clubs*—look for the following types of clubs, and if there are no clubs in a category your child is interested in, start one!

biology	robotics	programming
math	spelling	film
4-H	chemistry	Russian
television	Chinese art	investment
physics	jazz/choral	astronomy
cooking	genealogy	collectors (coin, stamp)
business	Shakespeare	book
travel	writing	art

- *Video documentaries*—view videos on the following topics for visual and auditory vicarious (indirect) experiences and discussion:

archaeology	astronomy	cinematography
geology	geography	anthropology
architecture	history	technology
machines	cultures	sculpture
artists	botany	banking

- *Performing arts*—witness the following in person or on YouTube:

ballet	mime	theater
opera	orchestra	symphony
chamber music	jazz	popular music

Read or attend the plays of famous playwrights, including the following:

Shakespeare	O'Henry	Chekov
Georgia Douglas Johnson		Arthur Miller

41

Read and discuss the work of famous novelists, including the following:

Lorraine Hansberry	Henrik Ibsen	Hildi Kang
Tennessee Williams	Amy Tan	Leslie Silko
Joseph Bruchak	Zora Neale Hurston	
Alexander Dumas	Miguel de Cervantes	
Mildred Taylor	Ryan Inzana	Janet Campbell Hale

- *Forms of transportation*—Give your child the experience of riding on some of the following:

animal (horse, elephant, camel, mule)		ship
train	taxi	bus
airplane	boat	bicycle
spaceship	airbus	blimp
covered or hay wagon	balloon	sled
snowshoes	skis	parachute
glider	rickshaw	hang glider

25. Use discussions to broaden your child's understanding of academic topics.

A discussion has the flexibility to take on a variety of forms. It can be a debate in which the parent takes a position and the child takes the opposite position; an exchange of ideas or opinions; or a give-and-take about a problem that needs to be solved.

To debate, select a controversial topic, such as climate change. You and your child can each pick a position or "side." Your positions will be in opposition, either for or against the topic. For example, one may argue that climate change is real while the other argues that climate change is imaginary. After the two of you have selected positions, tell your child each of you will find out, through research, at least five things to support your climate change position. Children love to debate in a friendly environment where manners are utilized, opinions are expressed without ridicule, and laughter is allowed. The point of your debate is to determine which position is more persuasive and better researched. That's where the fun comes in.

For an exchange of ideas and opinions, it is essential to first find out if your child knows what the topic is about. If he doesn't, suggest that both of you research the definition, characteristics, history, causes, and effects of the topic. Set a specific length of time for research. When the time expires, share your findings, ideas, and opinions. Reasoning and a little bit of emotion are allowed during this time. Don't forget that statements and responses to questions must be followed by supporting details—the justifications or reasons. Questions like the following help move the discussion along:

- Do you think climate change is real, imaginary, or exaggerated?
- Is studying climate change a waste of time or helpful?
- What could or should we as a family do with the information about climate change?
- How does the thought of climate change make you feel? Why?

Discourage one-word responses like yes, no, and maybe. You may say, "I like reading about climate change because the subject is not only interesting but also thought-provoking." Follow up by giving examples of interesting facts and some of your thoughts about your research: for example, the five years with the highest temperatures in recorded history and what this means to you.

Ask your child whether he likes or dislikes reading about climate change and why. A one-word or one-phrase response receives a reminder to share his newly researched information. If necessary, encourage him to repeat after you, "I [like / do not like] reading about climate change because ..." It may take a while to get a response like the one you model; however, do not be afraid to repeat your model or have the same discussion again. Remember, children learn through repetition and practice. Also remember consistency, composure, and commitment. If time is at a premium, suggest that the two of you continue the conversation later, but try to agree upon a specific day and time. You can also pose the most controversial questions first.

An opening to a discussion may be to ask your child about any researched findings that were surprising, entertaining, and/or thought-provoking, and then have him ask you questions about your statements, comments, and/or findings and what you found interesting and thought-provoking. Both of you should prepare and cite in advance at least three points to illustrate what was interesting and three to illustrate what was thought-provoking. Children find the out-of-the-ordinary very interesting, so to gain your child's interest and commitment to learning about and discussing a topic, look for the odd, strange, and unusual, and then introduce it.

Start by finding out what your child is studying in a particular subject, course, or class. Let's say he is studying the water cycle. You can ask about the causes of water shortages in areas of the country. Right now, attention is focused on California; however, there are other areas of the country functioning with water shortages. Could your area be affected by a severe water shortage? What could the family do if one did occur? What are the causes of water shortages anyway? There is plenty of water in the ocean, so what's the problem? Do not be surprised when you learn a few things yourself as you discuss the event. To discuss a problem that needs a solution, state what the problem is and then ask your child how the two of you might solve it. The next time, he states the problem and asks how you both may work on solving the problem. Discussions may focus on similarities (relationships/comparisons) between educational concepts and life, school, home events, past events, and/or future events.

26. Discuss current events.

Current events are a good way to help children understand and broaden their knowledge about a concept they will study or experience one day. Most if not all of the subjects a child learns in school are in some way reflected in current events, through documentaries (history, sciences, social science), the news (earth science, ecology, economics, geography, meteorology, sociology, sports), and the arts (political cartoons, painting, music, literature, cooking, poetry). When children pay little or no attention to current events, they may develop the notion that their lives have no connection to events outside of family or school, when in fact much of the gesturing in domestic politics, international economics, and foreign affairs has every bit to do with them and their future.

Pick a popular event in the news and draw your child's attention to how the event relates to him and to a school subject. As an example, you might discuss the federal minimum wage increase with your son. Through discussions on or reading about the federal minimum wage, he will broaden his experience with economics and social studies and learn how they affect him. The increase in the federal minimum (lowest possible) wage (money made by a person in exchange for his mental or physical labor) guarantees a working individual an income that (if he works an adequate number of hours per day, week, month, or year) allows him to meet his basic needs. Those "basic" needs vary based on geographical location. In North Carolina, the basic needs are food, shelter, utilities, transportation, and health care. Children love money talk, and the minimum wage offers an opportunity for parents to introduce real and vicarious (indirect) experiences in an academic subject, in this example economics / social studies.

To broaden the experience, you would have your child research the history of the event, including the preceding and recent circumstances that brought about the event. Hopefully, he will be open to further learning. In the example of minimum wage, questions that might be assigned include the following:

- What is the purpose of the minimum wage? (Possible answers: to send a message to the worker about the value of his labor; to protect workers from employers; to stabilize the economy; to provide a scale to evaluate work.)[16]
- Can a state have a different minimum wage? (Answer: yes, higher only.)
- Which state has the highest minimum wage? (Answer: Washington State, $9.32/hour. Minimum wage in Washington, DC, is $9.50/hour, but it is not a state.)
- Can a city have a higher minimum wage than its state? (Answer: yes, San Francisco, at $10.74, has the highest of all the cities in the country.)[17]
- How does minimum wage relate to you?

27. Have your child discuss with you what he is learning at school.

Children often do not have the opportunity to openly and freely talk outside of class about what they are learning. Discussion as described earlier offers opportunities for children to hear and listen to your ideas, evaluate their ideas in light of yours, and change their mind and/or modify their positions based on your questions and on the researched information they have gathered.

Give your child an opportunity to talk to you about what he is learning in school. At or after a meal or before he goes to bed may not be enough time for a discussion, so plan when, where, and how you are going to get your child to open up. Consider asking questions like the following:

- "What is the most exciting thing you learned in [school, math, history] this week?"
- "What is the most boring topic your [teacher, science teacher, social studies teacher] introduced this week?"
- "What did you learn this week that you found useful?"
- "What did you learn that made you happy? Made you think? Made you sad? Freaked you out? Made you feel as if you could save a part of the world?"

Generating questions can sometimes be more difficult than answering them. Fortunately, many books include a section of discussion questions at the end. Publisher or author websites often offer additional questions and material meant to supplement the reading.

When your child begins to share, ask a few questions or make statements to keep the conversation going, such as "Why do you find this topic so interesting?" or "I did not realize you were interested in _____!" The next set of questions should lead to further exploration of the topic: "Would you like to know more about the topic?" or "Would you consider making a living in an area related to this?" or "What can you do or contribute?" Follow up with something that will further your child's interest in the topic. A librarian or bookstore assistant should be able to recommend books or videos or both to improve children's understanding and broaden their experience.

If your child is repeatedly reluctant to discuss what was learned in school, schedule a teacher conference. Find out if your child is quiet or participates in activities. Many, many times, a child's behavior at home is exactly the opposite in school. Ask for suggestions.

Frequent discussions offer opportunities to examine, critique, and question the details of what your child is learning. Getting children to talk leads to their exploring the positives and negatives, correcting misconceptions, and refining their thoughts on the information they are learning.

28. Discuss with your child what *you* are learning, learned, or know.

If you are taking a course or reading for a degree, professional development, or pleasure, your child may benefit from your learning experience and your course's content. Do not be surprised to discover your child is learning concepts relating to topics in your course. Your educational experiences can enrich your child's knowledge base.

What you know can also come from your childhood, which is full of fascinating experiences you and only you can share with him. Think of the wealth of comical, emotional, and instructive stories about your extended family. Life then as now involved modes of transportation; means of financial support; importance of social and civic functions; periods of cooperation and conflict; and events of historic value. Your description of specific events, people, or items—like an old baby carriage, wrought iron toys, wooden rocking horses, and metal toy trucks—will capture the imagination of a curious youngster.

Don't stop there. Continue on with board games, housing, cars, televisions, radios, stoves, refrigerators, and other objects. If you have items from your past or memorabilia, that's great; if you do not, photos and images you find online can serve in that capacity. To children, the marked differences between today and yesterday's machines and gadgets and those from your or your parents' youth makes them seem like ancient history. Items in the attic collecting dust and looking ugly may offer stories and experiences beyond your child's imagination.

By 2018, no child will have been born in the 1900s. Our twenty-first century children will probably view anything invented or in existence in the twentieth century as ancient. Many items with which you are familiar, your children have had no experience with, yet in school they must learn about many of these things through maps, videos, and online newspapers.[18] If some elementary and middle school standardized achievement tests assess knowledge of the library's obsolete card catalog (circa 1870), which vanished circa 2004,[19] you can share much more than you realize.

29. Use information from your line of work to support what your child is learning.

The infamous schoolchild's query "When am I going to use this?" has the answer very near: your place of employment. Interesting information from your work may be used to explain concepts being taught in your child's courses. Your occupation probably requires a working knowledge of math, Standard English, science, or economics, each of which is taught in most grades. Fractions are used by carpenters; magnetism is in some rocks studied by geologists; sanitation is practiced by biologists; statistics are used by economists; chemical pigments are experimented with by painters; sales depend on the power of persuasion and extensive knowledge of your product; physics of sound is implemented by musicians; and the list goes on. Try to discover what your line of work involves that can be shared with your child.

Even if you are a stay-at-home parent, you can demonstrate for your child how basic lessons from school apply to everyday life. Fundamental math skills like manipulation of fractions, estimation, and multiplication are useful in shopping and paying bills. These and other skills make cooking easier. Color theory learned in art and size and shape learned in geometry are useful in decorating, while cooking and cleaning involve chemistry and physics. Many schools offer shop classes in which students can learn the basics of building and repairing things around the house as well.

30. Provide your child with national and international geography experiences (without actually traveling).

Today's geography courses include not only the physical terrain but also the cultural landscape. Reputable, high-quality magazines, websites, and videos have articles and graphics that provide colorful details of near and faraway places and people.

Without actually traveling there, your child can explore a continent's, country's, region's, or state's capital, landmarks, landscapes, currency, religion, dress, languages, customs, art, history, economy, and literature. Focus on one continent, country, region, or state at a time. Pictures, DVDs, and videos are available from the public library, while free or low-cost lectures, seminars, conferences, or film series are offered through local universities and colleges. Don't forget visitor's bureaus and welcome centers (free!), travel agencies, and travel magazines.

The following suggested sources may have subscriptions that grandparents are able to purchase as a holiday or birthday gift. If they ask what to give, suggest one of the following:

- *Scientific American,* http://www.scientificamerican.com/
- *National Geographic,* http://www.nationalgeographic.com
- *The Smithsonian*, http://www.si.edu/

31. Discuss the creation, purposes, and history of borders.

Recently, the US-Mexico border has been in the media quite a bit regarding illegal immigration. For a young child, lines of demarcation (borders) have no real meaning, but they can come alive while traveling by foot, horseback, car, bus, train, or plane and crossing the borders of parks, trails, shopping centers, neighborhoods, counties, cities, states, or regions. To broaden experiences in geography, history, culture, economics, ecology, and more, point out the borders to be crossed and explore the variety of reasons borders exist (possible answers include resources, separation, nationhood, treaties).

You can also point out that there was a time when borders did not exist; people believed land was God's gift to be shared by all. Ask your child why a border—much like a fence—would be necessary. Discuss reasons humans would want to keep some people in and some people out.

32. Expose your child to classics in music, literature, and art.

You may have to strike a bargain with your child over this one, but every child should be exposed to a variety of music and art forms from various cultures and times. The arts—visual, verbal, and performing—are among the most powerful forms of communication. Many of them speak across cultures, and even those that don't (meaning they require education for full appreciation) can serve as the start of a lesson about understanding others and even one's own place in the world. Unfortunately, not all teachers expose their students to the arts or use the arts as a teaching tool, perhaps because they fail to realize that the arts are potentially powerful communication vehicles. Children are drawn to the arts like magnets.

Tickets to arts events can be stocking stuffers or gifts (the kind of thing you can ask relatives give to your child instead of toys), especially since they may be expensive. Some performances can be accessed on the Internet for free, often on YouTube. Be on the lookout for freebies offered by arts councils and chambers of commerce, which are supported by your taxpayer dollars. Many philanthropic organizations purchase tickets in large numbers to be distributed to schools and low-income children.

It's important to stress that experiencing the arts with your children can create a much more rewarding experience for both of you. Conversations are easier when both of you know the subject well. The following are merely suggestions. Some are free, some are low cost, and some are expensive, so plan accordingly:

- *Every day*, play different classical music pieces (including jazz) as your child prepares for bed, straightens his room, and/or does his chores. Websites like Spotify.com and Pandora.com provide a variety of free music.
- *At least once a year*, treat your child to a play.
- *At least once every two years*, treat your child to a symphony.
- *At least once during elementary, middle, and/or high school*, treat your child to an opera.

33. Expose your child to Greek, Roman, Asian, and Native American mythologies.

Classics used to be a component of every child's school education. Though much less emphasized nowadays, the stories found in myths are still prominent in our culture. Going beyond the classics allows you to expose your child to the rich diversity of art in the world. But be careful! Many myths in their original form are X rated. Children's versions are available, although some may have been edited so heavily that they fail to resemble the originals.

Greek and Roman myths often appear as reading selections on standardized tests. The names of Greek and Roman gods like Adonis (used to describe a handsome man), Narcissus (used to characterize a person who is in love with himself), and Mercury (both the metal and, as the adjective *mercurial*, a descriptor meaning easily changed or changeable) form the basis for concepts used in English today, and thus should be learned as vocabulary words.

Children who are not exposed to Greek and Roman myths will be missing a basic level of information that informs many different subjects. Poets and painters have used myths as inspiration for some of the world's greatest artistic creations. Additionally, some standardized reading comprehension tests use references to mythology to assess both lower and higher level reading skills.

34. Take your child to ethnically diverse events.

Whatever you think about diversity, it is here to stay and your children will be—if they're not already—interacting with people from diverse backgrounds. Local arts councils, colleges, and universities often bring to the community culturally diverse events that are free and open to the public. If there is no culturally diverse programming in your immediate community, tap into the Internet or travel to a neighboring town that offers such programs. College towns are a good place to look.

The sounds and sights at these programs may be very different from those with which your child is familiar, and he may react with laughter, facial grimaces, or responses of surprise. Frequent exposure usually diminishes such culture shock. All cultures "shock" other cultures because the resources available within their geographical boundaries differ, and the people's views of life differ, including ideas about family, the roles of family and family members, community, nature, and the universe. Even on the same continent, there are variations in culture. Individuals may have preferences among and between cultures, but most anthropologists will tell you that one culture is no better than another. When one culture interacts with another, each culture learns from the other.

35. Consider diversity when encouraging your child to make friends.

Gross ignorance of and indifference to others is not a good place to be when the country is politically and economically dependent on "others" inside and outside of its borders. Making friends with a child whose native tongue is not English is a great way for your child to learn about another culture or language—and the learning can go both ways. Your child will benefit immensely from learning to speak at least one foreign language as well as knowing the rich history of that culture from its own perspective. Fluency in another language often guarantees employment in a highly competitive arena.

36. Explore and discuss diversity with your child, starting with his school materials.

A child's ability to respect cultural and ethnic diversity is more important today than ever. Exposure to difference has more than social, political, and economic benefits—it offers an intellectual boost. Respect for others can be increased when schoolchildren are taught that different groups have played significant roles in the greatness of this country and in the world, especially in science, mathematics, and technology—areas that demand thought, communication, and cooperation.

If you find little or no diversity in your child's school materials, share your findings with the principal. Take with you details like the title of the book, the publisher, and the ISBN number. You can and should also write a letter of complaint to both the author and the publisher of the text.

Supplement your child's materials with literature and graphics that tell the missing stories. For example, as a research project, have your child explore significant contributions females and different ethnicities have made in the subjects he is studying. Have him investigate how different cultures use the resources available to them to make clothing, use animals, and build homes.

As children learn about the differences between cultures, they may realize that most of the physical differences they see are produced by what is available in the people's environments. Thinking improves because an exposure to different viewpoints facilitates creativity. You want your child to be a divergent thinker—one who can develop solutions to problems—rather than a convergent thinker—one who follows directions developed by the divergent thinker.[20]

37. Examine values being put forth in school materials, textbooks, and handouts.

In education, nonacademic values instilled accidentally or deliberately fall under the category of "hidden curriculum," which includes the not-so-obvious values of punctuality, neatness, and respect for authority. Perhaps the most obvious of these values can be found in a school's disciplinary system. Regardless of the details, every school strives to cultivate in its students a sense of right and wrong, primarily in the form of honesty in schoolwork but also in how students treat others and themselves. Some schools even have students behave in accordance with an honor code that explicitly states these values.

Teachers stress the value of cooperative work when having students pair up or form in small groups for a project. Schools stress the value of authority both by the hierarchy of principals and teachers, but also by bringing in guest speakers to address topics that would often be outside the curriculum. Other values are less easy to spot, but are no less powerful. For example, if out of twenty scientists featured in a textbook, only three are women, a subliminal message is sent to students, female and male alike, that the field has little room for women, and the few women who do enter are not feminine (i.e., because they think like men they must be masculine).

To begin examining values presented in a textbook, look at the visuals. What do you see, and what do you *not* see? Is the information factual or opinionated? Has the evidence to support the information's validity been presented? Does the content attempt to persuade, and if so, for what purpose? Could the background of the author possibly bias or prejudice the work? In what way? Do omissions, distortions, and inaccuracies cause others to devalue those omitted or perceived as different? How are women and ethnic minorities treated—are they marginalized like second-class citizens, lower in rank and intelligence, or are they referenced as significant contributors to the knowledge base, leaders of flagship organizations, entrepreneurs who are amassing wealth, or solvers of major problem within their field? Biased, bigoted, xenophobic (fearful of strangers), racist, sexist, classist, or elitist ideas are often buried in texts, especially literary works, through roles, language, images, and omissions.

Women today—regardless of race, ethnicity, class, or income—maintain they are dismissed when attempting to contribute or overlooked for promotion or pay increase. Is it possible that subtle messages about women are buried in your child's textbooks? Such omissions, distortions, and inaccuracies offer opportunities to further your child's intellectual growth and economic capital.

38. Encourage your child to pursue a hobby.

In addition to constructively passing time, hobbies develop useful skills, reduce stress, provide topics for public speaking, and enhance applications for a job or college. One example of a hobby is constructing origami figures. Origami paper can be fancy and expensive or scrap paper and free. Origami helps a child construct angles, understand intersecting lines, create curves with flat paper, and see beauty in plainness.

39. Encourage middle and high school children to adopt a social issue.

Many of today's children fail to realize that participation in unpaid, socially conscious activities has educational benefits, such as learning different problem-solving techniques, hearing or witnessing human conditions and needs they may never have imagined, or experiencing satisfaction from helping another in need. Helping the less fortunate develops character and has appeal on a college application.

Although most agencies dealing with homelessness, poverty, hunger, sickness, and natural disasters provide volunteers with training before entering the setting, have your child research the history, causes, and impacts of a selected social issue to enhance understanding of the complexities surrounding the issue.

Another possibility for your high school child is joining a reputable organized group that addresses a social, political, or economic issue. Children should be taught how to participate in the democratic processes available to them in their communities. Engaging in a political, social, or economic activity enlivens concepts learned in civics, social studies, history, and economics. Your child's participation may also be likened to being "in the trenches," which wakens the practitioner to those times when theory (learned in the classroom) does not match reality (events in the field). Whether theory learned and reality experienced match or do not match, opportunities arise for very interesting family discussions and unforgettable memories.

40. Enroll your child in an academics-related workshop or summer camp.

As a part of recruitment programs designed to spark interest in their fields, many colleges, universities, and organizations (including NASA) conduct workshops or camps with attractive, fun-filled activities designed for elementary, middle, and high school children. One of the great things about these programs is their ability to show schoolchildren how schoolwork has application on the job, answering the well-known question children ask: "When am I going to use this?" These experiences may also help a child decide if he truly wants to work in a particular field.

The following are examples of these academic enrichment programs:

- UCLA K–12 Outreach, University of California, Los Angeles, http://www.k12outreach.ucla.edu/
- Children's Stage Adventures, New Hampshire Professional Theatre Association, http://www. childrensstageadventures.org
- NSBE Jr., National Society of Black Engineers, http://www. nsbe.org/NSBE-Jr/Welcome.aspx
- Envision Career and Leadership Programs, http://www. envisionexperience.com

41. Learn family history to pique your child's interest in history.

Learning family history as a family goal can be fun and educational. A client asked that we help her child improve her grades in history. No problem: her daughter would research her family's story.

We began by interviewing the oldest family members and then searched the genealogy section of the main library, with assistance from the librarian, to find anything listing family names. This section holds an array of offerings, from works listing real property which included human chattel to logs and itineraries of ships. In an old newspaper, she found a photograph of her father's great grandfather, who was a leader in his community—something her father did not know!

Meanwhile, her mother found her own grandmother's framed marriage certificate and asked why her grandmother would frame a marriage certificate. Answer: Enslaved Africans were not allowed to marry. After their freedom—and especially after the passage of the Fourteenth Amendment giving them citizenship—freedmen framed and proudly displayed their marriage certificates, letting guests know the couple was respectfully married. Her daughter learned much about the many hidden historical treasures in the family's background and developed an appreciation for history. Her grades improved too.

The ability to learn about family history has blossomed with the advent of the Internet. Sites like ancestry.com and ancestrylibrary.com provide web surfers with resources to investigate their own family's past. But the web has not replaced libraries—yet. Here are some of a library's assets:

- special collections, including books, quilts, and art
- copies of every book published in the United States, maybe not at your local library, but available through interlibrary loan
- quiet spaces
- technology for those who are without[21]

42. Prepare children for the places they will be visiting.

"Are we there yet?" is a question all children ask. Technology can come to the rescue, not only occupying time but also providing children with supplemental experiences in many academic subjects— including geography, biology, zoology, architecture, and foreign languages—while they travel to their destination. The Internet, e-books, audiobooks, and travel books from the library can be used to find facts about the history, folklore, flora, fauna, and terrain of the area they will be visiting. Together, the child or the family can explore the reasons (usually natural resources, climate, and/or culture) for the differences between and among geographic areas visited. As children travel, they can look for landmarks, historic buildings, and sites.

43. Give gifts that support academic learning and broaden experiences.

Telescopes, microscopes, gyroscopes, binoculars, construction kits, carpentry tools, stocks, and bonds—all offer not only opportunities to reinforce or experiment with concepts being taught in school but also a lot of academic fun. By the way, except for construction kits, the instruments may not be as expensive as you'd think. They also offer mentally and emotionally healthy alternatives to electronic devices. Information guides usually accompany the items; however, free experiments and activities for each can be found on the Internet.

44. Help your child develop imagination, creativity, and inventiveness.

By the time your middle school child enters the workforce, there will be thousands of skilled and highly skilled positions available. The newer types of work will require novel, creative, imaginative, and inventive approaches and ideas. Help your child develop his creativity and imagination with games and activities that require thinking outside the box. Many commercial games, such as Scrabble and chess, come to mind, but activities costing no money can also help your child develop creative thinking skills.

Jean Piaget—a biologist, psychologist, and researcher who developed the field of cognitive psychology by studying the logical thought patterns of young children—discovered that intellect and creativity develop when a child manipulates, handles, and plays using his hands, feet, and sometimes his entire body to feel and test an object's texture, size, shape, uses, and strength.[22] As Piaget did before, during, and after play, ask your child about his thoughts, intentions, and reasons for his successes and failures with objects. Simply by asking, you are helping your child reflect on his actions and take a step toward developing divergent, "out of the box" thinking. Activities like those that follow also help develop creativity:

- Send your child outside to play without anything other than his bare hands and tell him to play ball—without the ball.
- Engage your child in pretending to be a primitive child entertaining herself. Your child takes the lead; you follow. Remember, early human children did not have toys or games.
- Challenge your child to study the packaging from shipped items so that he can reconstruct the packaging after the contents have been removed. Many boxes have been ingeniously designed, so carefully separate the glued sections, unfold the flaps, and then flatten the box. Let your child reconstruct the packaging. After assisting with the first one, try your best not to help again so that your child is forced to imagine and visualize how the pieces fit together. Ceci's Pizza's grab-and-go boxes are an easy starting point. As your child gets better at rebuilding the containers, move up to more the difficult pieces and stop studying the box

before it is dismantled. Your child will learn to rely on his memory. This activity is especially good for a child who wishes to be a mechanical or architectural engineer.

- Introduce your child to origami, which involves the construction of art pieces without the use of tools other than the hands. Clean wastepaper, old notebook paper, gift wrap, magazine pages, newspapers, and paper bags (despite creases) will do just fine. The excellent website Origami Instructions (http://www.origami-instructions.com) posts free, step-by-step instructions for boxes, animals, flowers and more.
- Have a contest to see who can brainstorm more than fifty uses for a box, coat hanger, rope, or old shoe.

45. Encourage your child to solve problems without your help.

When your child asks your help with a fairly simple problem, such as a tangled cord of Christmas lights, ask what he has already done. After he has described perhaps three different attempts, pose questions or make statements that may cause him to explore solutions on his own: "Did you try …?" or "Think about …" Encourage him to continue. When he begins to whine, say, "You can do this! Try again." After fifteen to thirty minutes, if he has not solved the problem, he can stop, but have him return to the problem later, even if after a day or two.

As your child becomes accustomed to observing, tracing steps, and organizing thoughts, he should move toward greater independence in solving problems. Continue to be a coach, not a problem solver. Don't forget to praise him highly each time he successfully solves a problem. As he gets older, reduce the amount of praise so that he realizes that problem solving is expected and a way of life.

46. Intellectually challenge your child.

Experiences requiring a child to think outside the box yield great benefits for children growing up in a society where creativity, risk taking, and problem solving will be commonplace. Encourage your child's problem-solving abilities—especially by not giving solutions. Do the following as often as possible:

- Request two or more ways to solve the same problem.
- Require your child to tackle brainteasers and bonus questions teachers offer or textbooks or workbooks contain.
- Play problem-solving and risk-taking games, such as Clue.
- Encourage your child to develop games of his own.

47. Use chess to improve skills of observation, concentration, and strategizing.

Chess is a thinking game requiring observation, concentration, visualization, and time. If you don't know how to play, get an inexpensive set, read and follow the directions, go online to learn more about the game, and have fun as the entire family learns. Believe it or not, children can start learning chess at the age of three or four. Holidays, rainy days, and summertime are great times to start, because it may take you some time to learn the pieces and moves yourself. (Do not be surprised if your child learns more quickly than you!) Sets can be a inexpensive as five dollars.

48. Hold family tournaments.

Family is great for friendly competitions! Have atypical family reunions by conducting children's chess, math, history, and science tournaments. Nuclear family champions compete against the other nuclear family champions. Do this annually, and don't forget to award a trophy to the winner.

49. Make agriculture, botany, and biology come alive through gardening.

Expand your child's vocabulary and science knowledge with nonfiction (factual) books on gardening. Then, as he follows through with his task, have him read books on agriculture, botany, and biology to learn more about plants and to develop his vocabulary in selected content areas. Gardening does not require land or fancy pots—just seeds, dirt or sand, and a container like a cut-to-size milk carton that holds dirt and water. (Some of you may recall this activity from kindergarten and first grade.) Dollar and salvage stores sell inexpensive containers as well.

50. Teach your child *why* to eat specific healthy foods.

Parents can control what their younger children eat, but control over preteen and teen diets is almost impossible. To combat poor eating habits in later childhood and build experiences in nutrition and anatomy, teach your child in his early school years not only what to eat but also why those are good choices.

Food is the major source of nutrients needed for the health and proper functioning of specific body organs, cells, and organelles. One of the greatest negative impacts on learning and employment is illness, and the body uses vitamins and minerals in the following ways to avoid it:

- To protect cells, tissues (such as blood), and organs from toxins, the liver—the body's chemical plant—needs vitamins B2, B3, B12, C, and E; copper, manganese, selenium, zinc and sulfur.
- To promote learning and sharpness, the brain needs vitamins E, B12, and B6; folic acid; magnesium; and water.
- To prevent cavities, teeth need calcium and phosphorous.
- To prevent poor vision, eyes need vitamins A and C, lutein, and zeaxanthin.
- To prevent rickets, bones need vitamin D.
- To prevent anemia, blood vessels need iron, vitamin B12, and water.
- To prevent beriberi, the heart and nerves need vitamin B1 and thiamine.

Nutrients help the body heal when attacked.[23] For a further list of vitamins and their specific uses in the human body, visit the "Vitamins" page of the MedlinePlus Medical Encyclopedia from the US National Library of Medicine at http://www.nlm.nih.gov/medlineplus/ency/article/002399.htm.

51. Teach your child about money.

Before going off into the real world, children should have a foundation with money. Learning about money helps children of all ages understand several basic, everyday mathematics concepts that are sometimes difficult to grasp. When you shop, you may want to consider taking your child along, with the intention of discussing some of the real-life applications of mathematics, including the following:

- retail (the shop owner interfacing with the public) and wholesale (the provider of bulk products who interfaces with individual retailers)
- purchasing and selling
- unit pricing and discounting
- saving and budgeting
- borrowing and paying interest
- using credit

Comparison shopping and decision making are also involved. Consider allowing your elementary or middle school child to regularly work for you; your teenager to work a part-time job; or your child to operate his own business.

52. Use stocks to provide economics experiences.

Investing is not only an economics topic; it is also a math topic. Stocks are pieces of paper called *certificates* that attest to your partial (very small) ownership of a company and your share in the profits, if any, of that company. Bonds are also pieces of paper that attest to a loan you made to a company, city, or government agency, usually for the development of a product or the construction and/or repair of infrastructure. The amount loaned is repaid in full along with interest generated during the period of the loan.

Stocks and bonds are great stocking stuffers and birthday gifts. There are hundreds of stocks that cost just pennies (although penny stocks are risky and require research for a sound investment). Introducing your child to stocks is a fun way to develop personal financial awareness and responsibility while learning about a necessary investment tool. Your child should learn how stocks help small and large businesses energize the economy; how stocks may be tracked daily, weekly, or monthly to check on their growth or reduction in value; how graphing or charting your stocks' activities help you recognize trends; and how upturns and downturns in stock values are expected and not a cause for panic.

Find a broker who respects children's involvement in investing stocks, recommends stocks, and shows the child how to track and calculate profits and losses. Other facets of investment, such as researching companies, may be learned along the way. Your child may be able to participate in stock market games at school; visit http://stockmarketgame.org/impact.html and http://www. howthemarketworks.com to learn more about them.

Notes

16 Teresa Tritch, "F.D.R. Makes the Case for the Minimum Wage," *Taking Note* (blog), *New York Times*, March 7, 2014, http://takingnote.blogs. nytimes.com/2014/03/07/f-d-r-makes-the-case-for-the-minimum-wage/?php=true&_type=blogs&_r=0.

17 "Minimum Wage Ordinance (MWO)," Office of Labor Standards Enforcement, City and County of San Francisco, accessed April 26, 2015, http://sfgsa.org/index.aspx?page=411.

18 Bianca Male, "21 Things That Became Obsolete This Decade," *Business Insider*, December 11, 2009, http://www.businessinsider. com/21-things-that-became-obsolete-this-decade-2009-12?op=1.

19 Christine Frey, "Obsolete UW Card Catalogs for Sale," *Seattle Post-Intelligencer*, February 19, 2004, http://www.seattlepi.com/local/article/ Oboslete-UW-card-catlogs-for-sale-1137470.php.

20 "WOC STEM Conference," Career Communications Group, Inc., accessed April 26, 2015, http://www.womenofcolor.net; Christine Tachibana, "Diversity: Promoting New Perspectives," *Science*, July 20, 2012, http://sciencecareers.sciencemag.org/career_magazine/previous_issues/articles/2012_07_20/science.opms.r1200120; Toni Bernhardt, "What Type of Thinker Are You?" *Turning Straw Into Gold* (blog), *Psychology Today*, February 28, 2013, http://www.psychologytoday.com/blog/turning-straw-gold/201302/what-type-thinker-are-you.

21 Lee Rainie, "The Next Library and the People Who Will Use It," Pew Research Center's Internet and American Life Project, November 13, 2014, http://www.pewinternet.org/2014/11/13/the-next-library-and-the-people-who-will-use-it/.

22 "Jean Piaget," Biography.com, accessed January 22, 2016, http://www.biography.com/people/jean-piaget-9439915#synopsis.

23 "Vitamins," MedlinePlus Medical Encyclopedia, US National Library of Medicine, last modified February 2, 2015, http://www.nlm.nih.gov/medlineplus/ency/article/002399.htm.

Chapter 5

IMPROVING STUDY

Improving a child's academic performance depends on his ability to recall, think about, and apply the information learned, especially for tests. The suggestions herein are offered to help you become proactive in developing good, lifelong study habits in your child.

53. Check your child's ability to define the words he is required to read.

Many children, including older children, who struggle to grasp concepts have reading skill deficiencies. There are dozens of reading skills, but most poor readers suffer from weaknesses in sight vocabulary and general vocabulary. *Sight vocabulary* refers to the most frequently used words in both speaking and writing; they may not follow regular phonetic patterns and therefore must be memorized. Examples of sight vocabulary are *there*, *their* and *they're*, three words often confused by younger and older children. A list of sight vocabulary can be accessed online: search for "Fry's sight vocabulary." Ask your child to read aloud each word. If he misses or stumbles over any, have him learn to recognize and spell the word. Fry's compilation concentrates on the basic sight words, listing them in order of most frequent use.

You can use the vocabulary given to your child by his teachers. If your younger child is given spelling words only, take vocabulary words from his literature books. To find out if your child's general vocabulary is limited, take one of his textbooks or literature books, turn to any page, and have him point to or lightly circle with a pencil all the words he cannot understand or define immediately. Have him make vocabulary flash cards using index cards. On the unlined side, he will write the word in large letters. On the lined side, he writes the word again, along with its definition and a sentence using the word. The sentence should help him remember the definition of the word. For example, he may know someone who talks a lot. For the word *loquacious*, he might write, "Joan is loquacious."

If your child is unable to pronounce the unknown word, read the word to him as he looks at the word; have him repeat it to you and then spell it. If you do not know how to pronounce the word, use the Merriam-Webster online dictionary at http://www.merriam-webster.com, which has a pronunciation tool. Each night before bed, have your child read aloud and then silently each word and the definition. In the beginning, the number of words may seem overwhelming, but they become easier with practice. During sleep, his brain will review the vocabulary.

54. Ask questions to help increase your child's recall of information.

After your child has read his assignments, ask him to give you a summary of what he read. Children are usually very good at summarizing because many details may be omitted. Ask questions to find out his recall of details. Typical questions use the words *who*, *what*, *where*, *when*, *why*, and *how*:

- Who is the inventor?
- What is the definition?
- Where does the process occur?

- When is the next solar eclipse?
- How does the scene relate to the entire play?
- Who are the minor characters?
- What role does each play?
- Where do the events take place?
- When does the event take place?
- Why is the location important?
- How does the event help the learner?

55. Help your child with time management.

Many children do not know how to manage time, especially with respect to assignments, projects, and extracurricular activities. A study schedule (see #59) helps only if it is followed, and a homework assignment pad is useful only if assignments are recorded and then read. Thus parents may consider consequences for repeated forgetfulness. One alternative is to keep a copy of your child's study schedule posted on the fridge so that you know exactly what he is supposed to be studying.

A to-do list for each day of the week may help him manage his time. In the morning or the night before, he or the both of you can develop the list. Better still, have him develop it, and you check it afterward. On school nights, the list may consist of reminders for the next day's class, chores, homework, or equipment needed for an extracurricular activity. As with the tools mentioned earlier, the list is effective only if it is filled out and the items are checked off when completed, which may give him a feeling of accomplishment. Depending on the nature of the activity, whatever is not done one day should be attempted the next.

A school calendar may enable your child to organize or map out activities and deadlines in advance by week or month. If your child is extremely busy, consider limiting nonacademic activities to one or two per week.

Working backward is another planning strategy. Find the due date of an event—let's say a research report. Then have your child determine what has to be done immediately before submitting the final report to his teacher—usually typing the final draft, placing it in a folder or binder, and putting it in his book bag. The step before that is to have paper and ink supplies. Shopping may be necessary for these items, so shopping comes before actually having the items. Working backward works well for projects involving much detail or time.

56. Teach your child that deadlines are important.

Deadlines are organizational and time-management tools that demonstrate responsibility and help individuals achieve goals and objectives. They are a part of life. Your child may ignore deadlines because he believes they are silly, unimportant, or a restraint on his freedom, so point out that you, too, have deadlines to meet, from bill paying to employment demands. Explain that missing deadlines has a domino effect in the real world, perhaps using the following scenario:

- If you, the parent, submit your work late, the person expecting the report is unable to perform her duties.
- If she is unable to perform her duties, the company may lose a contract.
- Loss of a contract means the company cannot collect money.
- If the company cannot collect money, the boss must lay off people. Although there are different ways to determine who to lay off, the person who caused the backlog in the first place should be the first to go.
- If you, the parent, are laid off, then you are unable to receive a paycheck, which means you lack money to buy extras like games because basic needs must be met first.

Add that there are additional distasteful consequences if deadlines are not met, such as services being cut off, damage to one's reputation, and being tagged as a procrastinator, sloth, loafer, sluggard, slouch, deadbeat, and do-nothing. Reputation is important, especially if your child will need letters of recommendation for things like clubs and admission to college.

Most teachers have penalties for a late project or report, such as giving the student a zero on the assignment or dropping the grade by one full letter. Likewise, you, the parent, should levy a consequence for a missed school deadline. To help your child better understand, put a time limit on chores to be completed and impose a penalty when the task is undone and the time limit has expired.

Cleaning up a messy room is a chore for many children. First tell your child how you want items placed, arranged, folded, or stored. Be sure to have places to store the items. Then give him a specific amount of time—a deadline—to complete the task. If the room is disorderly by the designated time according to your verbal or written requirements, impose a penalty. If your child continues to disrespect timelines, consider denying his participation in an activity he truly enjoys until he adheres to your and his teacher's deadlines. Often one missed event does the trick.

57. Make no excuses for your child's failure to submit assignments on time.

Most teachers give adequate time for completion of assignments, so if your child missed a deadline—barring illness, family emergencies, and unexpected life events for which teachers often make allowances—investigate the causes. Unnecessary distractions like talking on the phone, procrastination, and disorganization are often at the root of incomplete assignments. Therefore, do not make, write, or call in an excuse for his irresponsibility. Let the penalty levied by the teacher be implemented. If you made a threat for not doing work, carry through, regardless of the penalty imposed by the teacher.

58. Do not help your child complete an assignment by assisting with or doing the work.

By the time your child reaches high school, he is supposed to be an independent learner, meaning he does not require supervision and independently assumes responsibility for his learning. If a parent repeatedly assists a child, the child is developing dependency. Some children, usually girls, ask for help by whining, crying, or insisting they cannot do or understand the assignments, and here comes Mama to the rescue. The habit is formed when you help him not once or twice but many times.

Ask the teacher if your child should be able to do the work independently or with adult assistance. Chances are quite good the work is supposed to be without your help. If that turns out to be the case, check to see if you caused your child to seek help.

If the teacher says he is supposed to receive help, ask why. Some assignments are intended to be a family project. If that is the case, she should have informed you of that as soon as the assignment was made. If you find you are helping your child because of the volume of homework, ask the teacher how long she thinks the assignment should take your child to complete. If she says an hour, then set aside an hour so that the assignment may be done without your help. Insist that your child complete the tasks within the hour, give or take ten to fifteen minutes.

Consider the impact of continuously helping your child:

- You rob him of practice needed to master the skill or concept.
- You rob him of developing responsibility.
- You rob him of becoming an independent learner.
- You rob him of becoming competitive in school and possibly the workforce.

- You learn the concepts and develop the skills instead of your child.

59. Establish a workable homework schedule.

Make a homework schedule, a time-management tool, with the five school days written horizontally across the top and the times vertically down the left side. Your middle or high school child, preferably without your assistance, fills in the subjects he is studying. For example, on Thursday nights, from six thirty to seven thirty, your child will do his math homework. You may have to assist an elementary school child with his schedule. After a few weeks, the schedule may have to be revised for omissions, additions, or reductions in days or times set aside. Each subject should have a specific block of time during which your child completes the task without interruption.

The length of assignments varies from teacher to teacher, subject to subject, or grade level to grade level, but time allotments can also vary from school to school or district to district. At the elementary level, some schools suggest twenty-minute set-asides for each course, which may mean assignments are so easy the child functions independently, without any kind of adult assistance. Others may suggest twenty to thirty minutes per subject. For a project, teachers may allot ten to thirty minutes each night over a period of time; hence, children should not wait until the last minute to do the work.

At the high school level, many teachers expect fifty to ninety minutes per subject per night. These assignments often involve extensive reading in addition to dozens of problems or questions. Some children may not finish until well after ten at night. These types of assignments are usually given to college-bound students.

When homework schedules work well, children know when and what they are supposed to study. Periodically monitor to see if the schedule is being followed and is working smoothly. If not, make the necessary modifications.

60. Consider banning study distractions on school days and school nights.

Related to time management are activities scheduled on school nights—Sunday through Thursday. On these nights, children should review class notes for the next day's classes, complete assignments, organize clothing and school materials, and plan lunches for the next day. Study time is limited, and children need to know this.

Distractions include but are not limited to games, videos, computers, phones, tablets, friends, social media, indoor and outdoor sounds (arguments, music, traffic, children playing, parties), and meetings. Strongly recommended is that you completely remove distractions—especially electronic game devices, and most especially if your child loses track of time and/or behaves as if addicted. Don't simply say these activities are forbidden on school nights and expect compliance. Remove them from his reach.

Of course, distracters may also serve as a reward for academic achievement. However, the reward should be given on the weekend, only because distractions interrupt concentration and cut into precious study time.

61. Encourage your child to compete against himself instead of others.

One way to develop an appropriate attitude toward learning is by having your child compete against his own academic performance instead of that of a sibling, friend, or classmate. As with athletes, the goal should be to break his own academic records. To do so, he must be aware of and work on his weaknesses. He may ask his teacher what he is doing incorrectly. A chart of scores on tests, quizzes, papers, and projects may greatly help him compete against himself. Make sure, however, that he does not put too much pressure on himself.

62. Teach your child to take good notes.

Starting in elementary school, teach your child to take notes, and make certain he knows how to take good notes by high school. Good high school notes may be useful with collegiate material.

Unfortunately, there are no tried-and-true ways to take notes. Some of the best recommendations are for the child to write a series of questions in his notepad, leave adequate space for the answers to be written, listen or read for the answers, and, when the answers are neither heard nor found, ask the teacher for the answers to the questions. For this method, the child must learn how to develop questions.

Start with a simple topic about which your child knows a lot: cars, ships, video games, and so on. Ask him to write down what, when, where, who, why, and how questions about his topic (no required order), each followed by a phrase about ships, for example.

The following sample questions are primary-level. Each question and response is a simple statement, written in a simple sentence:

- What is a ship? (Answer: According to Merriam-Webster, a ship is "a large boat used for traveling long distances over the sea."[24])
- Where are ships built? (Answer: A ship is built in a shipyard, a large area where workers and their equipment can move or be moved about easily.[25])
- When were the first ships made? (Answer: The first ships were made more than three thousand years BCE in Egypt and Mesopotamia.[26])
- How are ships used? (Answer: Ships are used for transporting people and cargo from one place to another, navigation of shallow and deep waters, warfare, defense, exploration, and pleasure.[27])

- How are today's ships made? (Answer: Shipbuilding is a complicated process involving designs by engineers and computer simulations.[28])
- Who made the first ships? (Answer: Egyptians made the first ships, followed by Phoenicians, Greeks, and Romans, not necessarily in that order.[29])

Possible sources for alternative answers to the above questions and more may be found at the following sites:

- Grades pre-K to 2: "All About Boats, Rafts, and Ships," http://easyscienceforkids.com/all-about-boats/
- Grades 3 to 6: "History of Transport and Travel," http://www.historyworld.net/wrldhis/PlainTextHistories.asp?historyid=ab79
- Grades 6 to 8: "Ancient and Modern Mariners," http://www.economist.com/news/christmas-specials/21636687-romance-high-seas-age-quantification-ancient-and-modern-mariners

As your child reads, have him write or type the words and definitions of the words he does not know and then answer the questions. These are sample middle-level questions:

- How is/are _____ similar to _____?
- How is/are _____ different from _____?
- What is the relationship between _____ and _____?
- What were the roles of _____ and _____?
- What is/was the role of the _____ in the _____ during the _____?
- What are the steps in the process?
- What are the characteristics of each step?
- How does each step differ from the previous step in the process?

Questions become more advanced when details are identified and comparisons are made:

- What evidence is there to support this concept?
- What are the salient (most outstanding, important, noticeable) characteristics of _____?
- Why is this information significant (important)?
- When and how will this information be used by me?
- What are the strengths and the weaknesses of the concept?

Sample high school questions:

- How do _____ and _____ compare (similarities and differences) economically (and/or historically, technologically, culturally, socially, politically, ethically)?
- Trace the development of transportation in the United States from the arrival of Europeans to the present day.
- Under what circumstances can the use of fossil fuels be justified in light of their negative impact on the environment?

The questioning method works well whenever notes are taken. The questions your child develops and answers also help him learn the material. Additional suggestions may be obtained from "Note-Taking Strategies and Skills" on the website TestTakingTips.com at http://www.testtakingtips.com/note/.

63. Have your child test or quiz himself after studying or completing assignments.

Developing a quiz actually helps your child learn the material. For the self-quiz, ask him to write five to ten questions. He can develop questions as he takes notes while reading the assigned text. Tell him to develop an answer sheet with the page number where he found the information. After finishing the assigned activity, ask him to take his test or quiz and then check his responses against his answer sheet.

64. Aim for perfect attendance.

Perfect attendance means your child will be present for all instruction. Whenever your child misses school, make certain he gets that day's lessons and assignments. Some teachers post their daily learning objectives and homework assignments on the school website. Some do not mind your calling them after school or at their home for the day's assignments. If your child will be absent for more than two days, let the teacher know; she may be willing to provide you with a packet of work.

Absences in kindergarten and the primary grades may have a negative impact on later school performance because the foundations of literacy (such as sight vocabulary, phonics, basic punctuation, and sentence structure) and math (number recognition, counting, addition, subtraction) are established during these years. The following page on the site of the National Center for Children in Poverty offers interesting, straightforward data about student absenteeism: http://www.nccp.org/publications/pub_771.html.

At any grade level, however, school absences usually impair learning and achievement. Reasons for absences vary from inadequate clothing for the weather to illness. If frequent and/ or an extended period of illness become an issue, see if there is a homebound teacher program that sends certified teachers to the home to provide instruction. A doctor's letter may be needed. Colleges and universities have students eager to tutor for a fee, college credit, or social responsibility. Inquire at the different college's departments.

65. Help your child learn and practice concepts in ways other than memorization.

Too many children memorize for a test and then forget the information. Instead, have your child explain, demonstrate, or illustrate concepts to you in one or more ways. The Tools for Educators site at http://www.toolsforeducators.com/crossword/ allows you to make crossword puzzles using definitions, terms, and vocabulary as prompts and answers. For other practice activities, have your child do the following:

- Write an explanation of how a math problem is solved.
- Draw a diagram of the scientific process.
- Draw a scene depicting his impressions of what he learned in social studies.
- Compose a poem, jingle, or short story about an event related to the assignment.
- Teach the concept to you or a sibling.

In preparing to teach, one often discovers the memory is unclear about one or more points. To help your child sharpen his memory, ask him to prepare to teach the concepts to you, forcing him to either reread or consult different sources that explain the concept. He can of course ask his teacher to explain again; it is better, however, to have the older child do his own research. A reputable, free online source is Khan Academy at https://www.khanacademy.org.

66. Encourage your child to use a variety of references.

Let your child know there are sources of information other than the encyclopedia. The ability to remember information may be enhanced if additional reputable sources are consulted, including professional organizations, such as the Native American Bar Association; governmental sites like NASA; university sites;

research organizations like the Centers for Disease Prevention and Control; reputable online magazines like *Science News* and *National Geographic*; and specialized libraries, such as the National Indian Law Library (http://www.narf.org/nill/index.html).

67. Make sure your child gets adequate sleep each night.

Studies on the impact of sleep on the learning process are revealing, especially for children. Many times children cannot remember how to perform a task or all the steps involved in performing the task, as in math, simply because they do not get enough sleep. A sleepy child in all likelihood will not perform optimally; his ability to listen or concentrate may be temporarily impaired. According to "Teacher's Guide: Information About Sleep" from the National Institutes of Health, teens should know the following about sleep:

- Growth takes place during sleep.
- More than eight hours of sleep each night is needed to maintain the ability to think clearly. (Note: the National Institutes of Health suggest nine hours for adolescents.)
- "Sleep loss causes problems with memory ... attention, complex thought ... performance in school ... and controlling emotions."[30]

68. If your child becomes sleepy while doing assignments, suggest a power nap.

Often a child becomes sleepy while doing homework, especially when reading assignments are long. When your child becomes drowsy, encourage him to get his energy boost from a fifteen to thirty minute nap. When he awakens, he will be able to continue where he left off. If your child repeatedly sleeps longer than ninety minutes, consider an earlier bedtime.[31]

69. Use technology to help your child learn.

More than ever, parents are able to help their children improve their academics with or without the help of professionals. Well-known providers of information for both youngsters and parents are on the Internet, including Discovery Channel (http://www.discovery.com), NASA (https://www.nasa.gov), Khan Academy (https://www.khanacademy.org), museums, and art galleries. Videos, audiobooks, e-books, and educational games assist with literacy, math, science, history, and foreign languages. They make great gifts too.

70. Make academic game cards for family fun—and studying.

The entire family may benefit from an academic quiz bowl. Make questions out of topics being studied in your child's classes, using things like vocabulary words, terms, names of people, titles, authors, places, dates, and events. On index cards, write a question on the blank side and an answer on the lined side. The fun derived from the competition should be adequate—but if desired, small, useful, inexpensive prizes like a notebook, pocket magnifying glass, or a novel eraser may be awarded.

71. Require your child to speak and write Standard English.

Many beginning writers often write what they would say in day-to-day speech, which may be slang, colloquialisms, or dialect. Dialects are variations of a language used in specific regions or by specific groups. Differences among dialects may be in grammar, vocabulary, and/or pronunciation. With a little effort, individuals speaking dialects of the same language can understand each other.

To be understood by people outside of the closed groups with which they frequently interact (school, neighborhood, family), children must learn to read, write, and speak Standard English, the only internationally recognized and instructional dialect of English. Standard English is spoken by leaders, teachers, reporters, meteorologists, and news anchors. All textbooks and standardized tests are written in Standard English.

Encourage your child to speak and write Standard English at home, everywhere, at all times. Let's face it: Standard English is the dialect of the bulk of books, newspapers, reference materials, and magazines; therefore, for effective communication in settings like school and work, Standard English is a necessity. To insist upon speaking a non-Standard dialect in school and in the workplace may be your child's ticket to the emerging underclass—and once in, it's very difficult to get out.

72. If your child has difficulty speaking Standard English, use strategies from programs in English as a Second Language (ESL).

ESL tapes, CDs, or DVDs—available in the local library—have been developed for the systematic, step-by-step learning of how to read, write, and speak Standard English. If your library does not have them, ask that they be ordered and to let you know when they arrive. Libraries can borrow materials from other libraries within the United States and beyond.

Aside from the library, an effective and easy-to-use model a parent may be able to use is the audio-lingual method, in which the parent structures or says a sentence or phrase to be repeated by her child. The sentence should come from a song, poem, or story—something with which the child is very familiar. Using the standard structures of a sentence from the work, the parent substitutes the nouns, adjectives, and verbs with others so that the child learns the standard structure of the sentence. The work probably has a variety of sentence types (simple, compound, complex), allowing the process to be repeated.

73. Give academic assignments whenever you think your child may benefit.

When school assignments take very little time or offer little challenge, consider giving your child academics-related assignments of your own. Assign a specific number of pages in a store-bought graded workbook; develop a weekly list of vocabulary words from textbooks; pick a literary work from the library to read and discuss by a specific date with you or the family; or request the solution to a set of math problems found online. Assignments may be given over the weekend as well—it's your call.

74. Consult the principal when your child's teacher falls short of expectations.

Needless to say, there are some teachers who fail to meet the academic needs of some children. The reasons may not relate to the teacher's inability to teach—there may be so-called "educational causes," including inadequate funding to purchase or repair needed equipment. If you believe your child's ability to learn and achieve is being jeopardized, meet with the teacher with the goal of sharing, discussing, and reducing your concerns with respect to your child's academic growth. Follow through on her suggestions.

If even then you are unable to see academic growth, you may wish to consult the assistant principal or principal. Realize, however, that the principal's hands may be tied; he may not be able to place your child in another class because of overcrowding, or he may not be able to release the teacher because of contractual agreements. Few schools are budgeted to hire a permanent substitute and pay out the expiring contract of a poorly performing teacher.

Although there is no guarantee, you may be able to negotiate the transfer of your child into another class. After politely presenting your evidence—copies of your child's declining work, attendance records, grade reports, and teacher comments via notes, e-mail, or texts—ask that your child be placed in another class. You may be fortunate to have a principal who is able to do so.

What else can you do? Find out from your child's teacher what she considers to be your child's weak areas, and look for a tutor with expertise in those areas. Consider the following sources for tutoring help:

- Most schools of education require a practicum in which the students perform free educational duties, such as tutoring or assessing.
- A church, sorority/fraternity, or local chapter of a professional or community-based organization will often offer academic support activities as a way of exercising social responsibility. (See, for example, the Sierra Club's environmental education offerings at http://vault.sierraclub.org/education/websites.asp.) Once the contact has been made, ask if the organization can possibly adopt your child's class; in fact, they may choose to adopt the entire school. First, though, out of courtesy, ask your child's teacher if she would like her class to be adopted by the organization for enrichment. Whether the class or the school is adopted, officials from the organization must get the written permission of the principal to perform tutoring services.

- Perhaps parents of children in your child's class would like to swap skills. For example, a nurse may be able to tutor in biology in exchange for your tutoring her children in areas related to your work. You may be surprised at the number of parents who would be interested in such a trade-off.

- If you are concerned about a location where tutoring can take place, consider booking a free room in the local library—or ask the principal or your pastor for use of a classroom or the fellowship hall. Your own apartment or house may work as well.

- Ask a librarian about tutoring services and other supports provided by the library, including DVDs in math, science, and history.

- Use an online tutoring service like Khan Academy (https://www.khanacademy.org. The Internet is filled with activities, lessons, practice, and guidance.

- If you liked one of your child's previous teachers or assistant teachers, ask if she would be interested in tutoring your child over the entire school year and even over summer. Offer modest compensation, which she may or may not decline.

- Consider college and high school students, especially those who would like to become teachers, as tutors. You may be able to find them through advertisements on supermarket, church, and local college or university departments' bulletin boards. Always check the tutor's credentials, references, and national and state criminal backgrounds (available from local police departments). Require the prospective tutors to provide these documents at their cost. The public library can serve as a tutoring site.

- Consider forming a support group. Parents often assume their child is the only one having difficulty with a teacher or with learning. Support groups can do exactly that—support parents whose children are suffering from poor teaching or learning habits. Ideas abound to help both parents and children.

75. Consult the principal when your child's teacher is frequently absent.

Teacher absenteeism and turnover put parents and principals in a difficult spot. Missed academic skills and lost instructional time need to be made up. Under the circumstances, you may respectfully ask the principal to set up tutoring services for the entire class through a neighboring college or university.

Record in writing your meeting dates, times, locations, those present, notes on the discussions with the principal, and the outcomes. You can ask if other parents have complained and what was done. The principal, however, does not have to respond to your questions, and his options may be limited by staffing issues or budgetary restrictions. Absenteeism may be caused by pregnancy, accidents, and illnesses, which are not grounds for removal and dismissal.

The terms of a contract may prevent the removal of an ineffective teacher, but when the contract expires, administrators usually take action—especially if the teacher is nontenured. Removal of a tenured teacher from the school system is a difficult process. Some states, such as California, are trying to find expeditious ways to release tenured teachers for unsatisfactory performance, which is not as easy to prove as one would think. Suffice it to say there is more to this particular battle than meets the eye and ear.[32]

Notes

24 "Ship," Merriam-Webster.com, accessed January 22, 2016, http://www. merriam-webster.com/dictionary/ship.

25 Alfred Pappas, "What Is a Shipyard?" SlideShare.net, accessed January 22, 2016, http://www.slideshare.net/AlfredPappas/what-is-a-shipyard.

26 "History of Boats and Ships," History World, accessed January 22, 2016, http://www.historyworld.net/wrldhis/PlainTextHistories. asp?historyid=aa14.

27 "Different Types of Ship in the World Merchant Fleet," International Chamber of Shipping, accessed January 22, 2016, http://www. ics-shipping.org/shipping-facts/shipping-and-world-trade/ different-types-of-ship-in-the-world-merchant-fleet.

28 "Oil Tanker Ships," *How It's Made*, ScienceChannel.com, accessed January 22, 2016, http://www.sciencechannel.com/tv-shows/how-its-made/videos/how-its-made-oil-tanker-ships/; Cuthbert Coulson Pounder, "Ship Construction," *Encyclopædia Britannica*, last updated January 22, 2015, http://www.britannica.com/technology/ship-construction.

29 "History of Sailing Ships," *Ships and Boats*, Q-files, accessed January 22, 2016, https://www.q-files.com/technology/ships-and-boats/ history-of-sailing-ships/.

30 "Teacher's Guide: Information About Sleep," *Sleep, Sleep Disorders, and Biological Rhythms*, National Institutes of Health, accessed April 29, 2015, https://science.education.nih.gov/supplements/nih3/sleep/guide/info-sleep.html; Marija Bakotić, Biserka Radošević-Vidaček, and Adrijana Košćec, "Educating Adolescents About Healthy Sleep: Experimental Study of Effectiveness of Educational Leaflet," *Croatian Medical Journal* 50, no. 2 (April 2009): 174–181, http://www.ncbi.nlm.nih.gov/pmc/ articles/PMC2681062/; "Brain Basics: Understanding Sleep." National Institute of Neurological Disorders and Stroke (NINDS), last modified July 25, 2014, http://www.ninds.nih.gov/disorders/brain_basics/ understanding_sleep.htm; Sarah Graham, "Experiment Shows You Should Really 'Sleep on It,'" *Scientific American*, January 2, 2004, http:// www.scientificamerican.com/article.cfm?id=experiment-shows-you-real.

31 "Vitamins," MedlinePlus Medical Encyclopedia, US National Library of Medicine, accessed April 29, 2015, http://www.nlm.nih.gov/medlineplus/ ency/article/002399.htm; Jennifer Soong, "The Secret (and Surprising) Power of Naps," WebMD, accessed April 29, 2015, http://www.webmd. com/balance/features/the-secret-and-surprising-power-of-naps.

32 Valerie Strauss, "The Problem with the 'Problem with Tenure' for Teachers," *Answer Sheet* (blog), *Washington Post*, August 26, 2014, http://www.washingtonpost.com/blogs/answer-sheet/wp/2014/08/26/ the-problem-with-the-problem-with-tenure-for-teachers/; Matthias Gafni, "Firing a Tenured Teacher in California Can Be Tough," *San Jose*

Mercury News. January 26, 2013, http://www.mercurynews.com/news/ ci_22454531/firing-tenured-teacher-california-can-be-tough; Marcus Winters, "Tackling NY Teacher Tenure," August 25, 2012, http://nypost. com/2012/08/25/tackling-ny-teacher-tenure/.

Chapter 6

HANDLING EMOTIONS RELATED TO SCHOOL AND LEARNING

When children are struggling to establish and maintain their self-confidence, self-respect, and self-awareness, your three Cs (composure, consistency, and commitment) may be tested many, many times. You may also experience great emotional stress. Maintaining your composure during these stressful events is imperative. Refer back to chapter 1—especially #3, on creating a proactive rather than a reactive environment—for further discussion. This section addresses what may be done to help you handle the emotional upset children often experience when their studies are not going as well as they, or you, had planned. Recommendations relate to developing an emotionally, socially, and academically well-adjusted child.

76. Create a warm, receptive, affirming environment.

Children are interesting creatures. They are vulnerable and dependent upon an adult for their survival, and they know it—yet sometimes, they act as if you need them more than they need you. As the adult, you know they will eventually need you. Although most of their life experiences will offer physical, mental, emotional, social, and intellectual benefits, some will be unpleasant and difficult to understand or manage. When the negatives hit, it is extremely important that the environment and communication you have created allow them to share with you not only the good but also the bad and the ugly.

You will be dealing with hurt and confusion, so aim for an environment and communication free of yelling, name-calling, disorganization, and expressions of dislike, contempt, and hate.

Also eliminate words and actions that are destructive, hurtful, argumentative, violent, discouraging, and hindering. These are and have been obstacles you deliberately placed or allowed others to place in your children's developmental path.

If your environment is negative, conduct as many family meetings as are needed to change behaviors for the sake of everyone's health. Iron out what is acceptable and unacceptable behavior and what the consequences will be for breaking the family's behavior code. You, the parent, should be the primary model. Admit to the family that changing bad behaviors will not be easy and that the process will be gradual, but it is for everyone's betterment.

77. Be on the lookout for symptoms of emotional distress.

When children have problems in school, rather than telling their parents about their distress or difficulty, they may do one or more of the following:

- make frequent negative utterances about themselves, others, and/or their environment
- repeatedly refuse to try to do a household or academic task
- experience a sudden drop in grades
- state that others are better or smarter
- display antisocial behavior like bullying, fighting, or isolating self from others
- have more angry outbursts than usual
- joke or fool around excessively
- frequently complain about stomachaches and headaches
- ask to stay home from school
- suddenly or gradually lose broad smiles and cheery disposition
- change in personal hygiene or appearance
- daydream excessively
- suddenly change personality

The symptoms listed require attention. Ask your child if he is having any difficulty—behavioral, social, or academic—in school. Regardless of the response, make an appointment with the teacher to determine for yourself if something is taking place that you should know about. You may wish to shadow your child throughout an entire school day so that you get a complete picture. If there is no informative feedback and the actions persist, seek professional help. Consult social services for free counseling.

Begin with a thorough medical checkup. The doctor will make a referral if she finds no medical reason for the sudden changes in behavior and if she thinks your child may benefit from counseling. If medication comes up in discussions anywhere, before consenting to have your child medicated, ask for written and verbal general information on the immediate and long-term effects the drug will have on your child's physical activity, sleep, eating habits, moods, and emotions. Ask specifically about immediate and long-term effects of the drug on fertility, concentration, and overall health, now and in adulthood. The answers may cause you to reconsider.

78. Communicate your emotional support through action.

Sometimes parents do not know how to communicate emotional support. Try the following suggestions:

- Pin an encouraging note where your child can see it every day.
- Encourage, praise, hug, and smile at your child every day.
- Engage in active listening by periodically nodding your head or making a response, even one as brief as "Really!" or "Uh huh."

- Express empathy by saying as your child speaks, "I can only imagine how you felt" or "You must have felt terrible" or "I wish I had been there to share your joy/hurt."
- Keep the promises you make.

Parents are often quite busy with their professional and social obligations; however, children's needs should come first, so do your very best not to disappoint your child when you have made a verbal commitment to do something together. Many states and businesses now recognize the importance to parents of addressing the needs of their minor children. Find out if you can take time off to tend to your child. Use that time to keep promises you made; treat those promises as obligations. If you must postpone the engagement, explain that you will satisfy your verbal contract at an alternative specific time, place, or date—and keep the appointment. Remember, it does not take much to make a child happy. Try the following simple gestures:

- Take time out to discuss with your child his feelings about his academic progress or lack of progress; strengths and weaknesses; and nonacademic successes and difficulties.
- Encourage (but don't demand) mastery of an academic or nonacademic problem, skill, or task.
- Positively recognize each step your child takes that gets him closer to mastery.
- Praise or reward mastery of a problem.
- Give a daily dose of hugs, smiles, and encouragement.
- Tell him he is a great kid.
- Tell him you are very proud to be his mom, you're happy he is your child, or you could not have had a better child.
- Share with him something that results in a hearty laugh, like a funny video, joke, or recollection.

79. Help your child handle frustration.

Unfortunately, frustration is a part of life, and for sound mental health children must learn how to deal with it. Both good and poor students experience frustration at some point. Your child must develop an ability to identify frustration and handle it appropriately. Meet both frustration and anger with respectful responses, empathy (you have experienced frustration yourself and know how it feels), and helpful suggestions.

Your child's frustration may be signaled by frequent rubbing or scratching of head, eyes, or hands; deep sighs or forceful blowing of air from the mouth; frequent staring into space; constant shaking of one or both legs; or often putting the head down, perhaps falling asleep. When you notice these actions, gently ask questions like "Having difficulty?" or "Is what you are working on a little tough?" If your child answers in the affirmative, follow up with "What's causing the frustration?" If your child is able to tell you what the problem is, great! If not, you must help in making that determination.

Below is a partial list of verbalized and common sources of children's frustration that may help you pinpoint the source. Turn each into a question until your child responds in the affirmative. If the cause remains unidentified, have your child note what happened just before the frustration descended. Tell your child to write down what preceded the feeling whenever frustration recurs. Identifying the cause of frustration helps you help your child develop a constructive solution. To adults, this list may seem ridiculous; however, to a child who does not yet think like an adult, the following events feel like a big deal:

- repeated difficulty with vocabulary
- repeated inability to understand the text
- repeated inability to understand the teacher
- repeated inability to do the assignments
- repeated miscalculation of problems

- repeated misinterpretations of stories
- repeated discomfort with strategies to solve a problem
- uncertainty with the steps in a process
- repeated misunderstandings with peers and parents
- repeated errors made on a quiz, test, class work, or homework

You may have missed earlier signs of frustration if your child exhibits any of the more noticeable behaviors, such as whining, crying, yelling, hitting, kicking, punching (objects or others), destroying things, or avoiding work. If he shows anger, insist he take a break from the situation by participating in a brief physical activity until he feels better or more relaxed. He probably knows anger is bad, but he may not realize the damage being done to his health, especially his heart, by the release of the hormone cortisol. Frequent anger often leads to high blood pressure, stroke, or heart attack.[33]

Help your child develop a solution to the problem. For example, if an inability to understand the text is frustrating him, a possible solution is to have him scan the text for unfamiliar vocabulary words, which he then defines. Next he rereads the text, replacing each unfamiliar word with a familiar synonym or definition. To avoid continued frustration, he should learn the definitions. Perhaps you can follow up by quizzing him.

Lastly, have your child review and rehearse the steps followed to deal with frustration so that when it rises again, he'll know what to do: identify the problem, find a solution, apply the solution, and take steps to prevent a recurrence.

If your child's teacher is the root of his frustration, schedule a parent-teacher conference. Find out from your child exactly what the teacher says or does that is upsetting. Keep in mind there are always two sides to the story. Maintain an open mind and listen carefully.

If there is no resolution, you may consult the guidance counselor or the assistant principal before going to the principal. You may ask the principal if other parents have expressed difficulties with the same teacher. If the answer is yes, ask what he will do about it. He may not share his plan for administrative reasons, but your asking lets him know he may have a more serious problem if he does not act. He must honor the teacher's contract, so do not expect her to disappear overnight.

80. Share a few frustrations you have experienced or are experiencing at work.

When your child comes home looking and feeling as if the world is on his shoulders, he needs understanding, encouragement, and inspiration. Most children will have at least one rough day in school for any number of reasons—such as a teacher or classmate speaking rudely to him, an unsatisfactory grade on a quiz or test, a newly introduced concept he does not yet understand, or lost instructional time because his teacher is frequently absent. To help him learn ways to handle his difficulties, share with him one or more of your rough days at work or at home, such as a task that did not go as planned or a new assignment unexpectedly dropped on your desk. Share the stress it caused and how you handled your frustration.

Identifying the cause of the frustration is a first step. Eliminating the cause of the frustration is the second. Healthy strategies for stress reduction include physical exercise, prayer, writing about the incident in a journal, or talking it over with a friend or relative.

81. If your child's anger results in violence or dropping out, consider pulling him out of the school immediately.

Some children become very angry when their academic or intellectual needs are not being met. Causes of their lack of achievement can range from boredom to a lack of skills, from bullying to addiction. Taunts, shame, embarrassment, and humiliation—especially in front of classmates—often make matters worse. These children are at risk of dropping out, either mentally or physically. They need special attention a regular classroom teacher may be unable to give, even if she can recognize the distress. For these children, dropping out becomes a viable mechanism for escaping pain and discomfort. Often, their ego and self-confidence have been damaged.

Radical changes in behavior—such as becoming very quiet, withdrawn, or talkative—need attention. Other calls for help are frequent complaints of stomachaches or headaches; onset of bedwetting or excessive eating; and references to violence in speech, essays, journals, or artwork. Without appropriate, helpful outlets, there may be only so much your child can take, so he explodes with angry outbursts, destroys property, or vandalizes the classroom—or implodes by harming himself. Whether exploding or imploding, your child needs to be immediately removed from this educational environment and placed in one where his needs can be professionally met.

If you are unable to find a school equipped to help your child, investigate homeschooling in your state and area. The resources available may be surprising. Online education and tutoring via Skype are also possibilities. Don't let the school-to-prison pipeline suck up your child.[34]

82. Do not give up on your retained child, and do not let him give up on himself.

Often we get children who have been threatened with retention or have been retained, sometimes more than once. Do not assume your child is dumb, stupid, or slow. He is probably neither, so do not despair. He needs you! An article in *Science News* on a study done with children who survived catastrophic disasters like earthquakes presented suggestions that are not surprising: keep the child close, speak calmly and comfortingly to the child, and remember that the human touch is important. Warmth in your voice and gestures give the child a sense of stability and feelings of security and comfort.[35] No, the pain cannot be immediately removed, but with lots of time and appropriate strategies, it will subside. The lesson is that when a child is retained, parents must be calm and comforting. You will also need comforting, because retention is stressful for parents too.

Both of you need hope and a plan. Do not place blame; rather, try to find what failed your child. Was it the school, the curriculum, the instruction, the teacher, friends, the neighborhood, an absent parent, social media, bullying, a loss? Look for more than one thing, because rarely does only one factor fail a child.

To calm and comfort your child, talk in a simple and nurturing way. Stress that there are solutions. Address literacy skills, because all too often they are at the root of school failure. Literacy is extremely important, not only for academic achievement but also for social development and advancement. Children can be cruel; once they discover a classmate cannot read, belittlement and ridicule strike with the sharpness of a razor, leaving deep, permanent scars.

It is rare for literacy issues to disappear by themselves. Professional help may be needed. Ask the guidance counselor for resources. Ask the church congregation if there are any retired teachers willing to tutor. Research homeschooling as a viable option. Among literacy skills are study skills, which should also be investigated (see chapter 5).

If literacy is not an issue, investigate your child's friends. While friends are supposed to be supportive, some children confuse friendship with their felt need to belong to a group of peers. These children often select those who offer destructive speech and interactions: they isolate, ostracize, humiliate, and haze. If that is the case, a change in friends is needed. If your child is young, you make the necessary changes. If your child is older, you may have to find ways to get your child to make this decision. Now, seek remedies: literacy instruction, intensive tutoring, change in friends, change in study behaviors and patterns, or homeschooling.

83. Make certain your child's wants do not get in the way of his needs.

Children often come home asking parents to purchase items other children have. Stick to your guns. If your child objects to your decision not to honor the request, give your reasons, which may include that fact that the item is unnecessary and costly. Many children do not understand the difference between a need and a want. Others do not understand that money should not be spent before it has been received.

To make certain your child begins to develop financial literacy, define a *need* as a must for survival—something that, without it, his health and perhaps life are in jeopardy. A *want* is something he would like to have for pleasure or comfort or because others have it. In economics, needs must come before wants. Water, food, shelter, utilities, health care, transportation, and (for children) education are needs. Believe it or not, there are children who believe they can live quite comfortably without knowing how to read and calculate, despite hearing that jobs for unskilled labor are becoming fewer in number and that those who cannot earn enough money to eat and pay rent often become homeless or turn to illegal activities. Unfortunately, these children wrongly assume yesterday's and today's job markets will be exactly the same in the future. Equally unfortunate, many of the children are surrounded by gainfully employed, comfortable adults who are illiterate or uneducated, many of whom believe an education is a waste of time.

Use the following list of choices to help your child tell the difference between wants and needs (needs are italicized):

- *food* or a video game
- *medical checkup* or a trip to a video arcade
- *a safe place to sleep* or a pillow
- a bed or *a blanket*
- spending time on Facebook / Snapchat / Twitter / cell phone or *spending time on homework*
- dessert or *a nutritious breakfast*
- a favorite shirt or *a warm coat for the winter*
- *a textbook* or a favorite (computer) game/sport
- a "cool" car or *a means of getting to school, including walking*
- a bed or *a safe place to sleep*
- three pairs of pants or *one pair of pants*
- *one pair of shoes* or a pair of bedroom slippers
- a bedroom or *a safe place to sleep*
- *a high school diploma* or twelve trips to amusement and/or sporting events
- a conversation about sports with a friend or *a completed math homework assignment*
- a can of soda or *a glass of water*
- *a serving of a green vegetable* or a bag of potato chips
- a birthday party or *school clothes*
- *an orange* or fruit punch
- a summer cruise or *heat in the winter*

- drawing classes or *literacy tutoring*
- bedroom accessories or *school supplies*
- *heat/air-conditioning* or signature sportswear
- *saving for college tuition* or saving for trips to Disney World
- school supplies or *food* (many people, including teachers, do not realize some families must make this decision daily)
- *studying for a test* or attending a party

Make modifications to these choices to fit your and your child's specific situation. Next, write each of the pairs of choices on either a slip of paper or an index card. On a board or notebook paper, draw two columns. Label one column "Needs" and the other "Wants." Ask your child to select and write one item in the pair that is a need in the needs column. The remaining item is placed or written under wants.

Some choices are deliberately difficult, but your child must make a choice. Don't forget to discuss the correct answers and your moral and/or legal responsibility as a parent to meet his needs first and his wants second. Emphasize that wants are always both an option and your decision—and that providing the needs at times can be a true struggle.

Economically speaking, a bed, sheets, pillows, rugs, curtains, bedroom furniture, games, toys, and trips fall under wants, not needs. A bedroom is not a need, but a relatively safe place to sleep is (although some municipalities have specific laws about bedrooms and the number of persons and gender of those persons sleeping in those rooms). A pillow is not a need, but for health a cover of some type is. Desserts or snacks are not needs, but for nutrition a balanced meal is. Two, three, or more pairs of pants, socks, shoes, and boots are not needs, but for health and safety protective clothing is. Entertainment is not a need, but for communication, civic, and economic responsibilities, an education from ages seven through sixteen is.

If your child does not already know, tell him that parents providing their children with the basic necessities of life—water, food, utilities, shelter, medical care, transportation, and access to a school—are being responsible. Tell him everything beyond the basic necessities is a gift from you. He must know the difference between a need and a want so that he can put your responsibilities to him in perspective and rethink his responsibilities to himself. His wants may be used to direct, guide, and channel his academic and physical behaviors in and out of school.

84. Explain to your child the difference between his and your legal rights.

Ask your youngster (age seven through fourteen) what he thinks his rights are by law. Question his assumptions about the consequences that should be levied against you for not giving him what he wants or what his friends and playmates have. He may express shock or disbelief when he learns you are not obligated to provide toys, games, electronic devices, fashionable clothing, and/or an allowance. From these invalid assumptions, he may conclude you are abusive, irresponsible, spiteful, or mean when he does not get his way. He may think he should report your abuse to school personnel or the police.

Your child needs to know he has no right to gifts, and when he receives them you have the right to take them away. A shocker to him may be that you have a right to any money—including child support—he has saved, earned (child actors are exempt and in a different class), or been given. By extension, whatever he purchases with his money is a parental gift and can be taken, returned, or withheld by you, and he has no legal way to get the items back. He has a right to be clean and presentable to the public but no right to sweet-smelling soaps, colognes, and lotions. He has a right to be groomed but not by a beautician or a barber. He has a right to an education but no legal right to an excellent or private education or tutors. Needs and wants cost money. There is no free lunch.

Parents have to remind children that they have a legal responsibility as parents to provide children with what they need, not what they want. Parents need to know that when they provide their children with the basic necessities of life—water, food, shelter, clothing, medical care, and access to an education—they are being morally, socially, and legally responsible. Rights provide parents with leverage to rear children—for example, withholding or removing a prized or desired want, such as a toy, is often used to redirect misbehavior or encourage better academic habits.[36]

Note: There are instances of homeless parents being subjected to threats of losing their children to foster care by court judges and child welfare and homeless assistance agencies.[37]

85. Ensure your child is practicing daily good personal hygiene.

Children in general and boys in particular are notorious for neglecting their hygiene by wearing unclean clothes, avoiding baths, skipping toothbrushing and hair combing, forgetting deodorant, and failing to wash their hands after using the bathroom.

Poor personal hygiene invites ridicule. Children, including the very young, can be cruel to each other, especially when they smell odors on another. To keep your child from being teased, embarrassed, or humiliated, make certain he develops habits that foster good health and hygiene.

The bed wetter and thumb sucker require special attention to avoid being shamed. Check daily to see that the bed wetter bathes and dons a complete set of clean clothes, and that the soiled clothing and linens are thoroughly cleaned. If he is seven or older, consider having him strip the bed and wash and dry his soiled linens—and take him to the doctor to make sure this is only a bad habit that must be broken. Thumb suckers have to make certain their breath smells fresh not only by brushing their teeth regularly but also by rinsing morning and evening with a good mouthwash.

Some schools have restrooms in the classrooms. If so, teach your child to courtesy flush—flushing immediately after the feces exits the body. The odor as well as the distraction it causes is greatly reduced.

86. Be sure your child practices good manners and self-control.

Teaching appropriate social interactions should never be left up to the schools; school is where social interactions are practiced. Most parents teach their child the difference between right and wrong as well as respect for others—which should not include hitting back when a child accidentally or deliberately hits. Classrooms and schoolyards are not combat zones; they are places where children learn to interact civilly with one another. When a child has no manners, more than a few teachers assume the worst about the child and his family.

For example, a teacher was overheard saying to other teachers that a particular child "will never contribute to society," "will probably grow up to be a criminal," and has "parents who are uncaring, negligent." Considering literature on teacher expectations, the child's teacher's expectations may be so low that her language, behaviors, and choices toward and for the child in all likelihood will result in extremely poor academic achievement by the child.

87. Handle bullying effectively and efficiently.

Effectiveness relates to achieving the desired outcome: an end to bullying. Efficiency relates to skillfulness in getting the task done: immediately or as soon as possible. If the bullying is in school, have your child provide you with the following details:

- date
- time
- name of the teacher in charge
- location of the incident
- name of the offending child
- what the offending child said and/or did
- names of any witnesses.

Take the information to the child's teacher and tell her you want the bullying stopped immediately. If she asks for suggestions, tell her that is not your responsibility and that you will ask within two days what she has done to bring the bullying to a halt. Contact her to find out what she did.

If the bullying happens again, when you are composed tell both the teacher and the principal that you will let the superintendent settle the matter if they cannot. Then do so. If the bullying happens again, let the teacher, principal, and superintendent know you will take the matter to the police.

Ideally, at the end of the first conference, the teacher and principal will tell you they will address the bullying immediately. Ask them how they intend to do that. If they say they will get back to you, tell them the bullying may happen again the next school day, and your child does not have time to wait. There should already be a policy in place, and you want to know what it is and why they did not promptly implement it. Mention witnesses, dates, times, and locations. When the principal hears those details, he should know legal action is an option for you. Acting and speaking in a composed and reasonable way will work to your benefit.

If bullying takes place in the neighborhood, a similar approach can be used. For your records, describe in writing the bullying incident. Include details like the following:

- date
- time

- location
- bully's name
- what was said and done
- bully's parents' names, if known
- names of any witnesses

Politely let the parent know her child is bullying your child and state that you would like it stopped immediately. Mention specific times, dates, and witnesses so that she can approach her child with the facts of the accusation.

The bully's parent should thank you for letting her know what her child has been doing. Often a parent is completely unaware of her child's abusive behaviors; she probably thinks he is an angel. If the bullying happens again, let the parent know, but this time tell her you will take the matter to the police if it happens once more. If your child is bullied again, follow through with your threat.

Unfortunately, there are times when a parent does not respond as expected to a negative report about her child. When this happens, say or do nothing other than leave immediately. Do not get into an argument. Walk away. If the bullying happens again, call the police, file a complaint, and take the officer's advice. Be sure to let the officer know the bully's parent was hostile.

If your child is the bully, you must address his behavior immediately. Present him with the facts that you have. Discuss his reasons for bullying, but make it clear that there are no justifications for bad behavior. You may wish to view with your child this video on the *Huffington Post* website about a bully who changed his ways: http://www.huffingtonpost.com/2014/05/27/cameron-thompson-bully-club_n_5395664.html.[38]

Sometimes a child has no idea why he bullies but has feelings inside that powerfully urge him on. Those feelings are physically destructive to his health, and you must let him know that. Many reasons for bullying are emotional, and youngsters often do not know how to handle their issues. Causes of bullying may be frightening, but as the parent of a bully, you must explore them.[39]

Ask your child if he is aware of what can happen to him if he continues to act in his chosen manner. He will probably say he is unaware; let him know bullying may be a criminal offense. You and your child should then visit http://www.stopbullying.gov/laws/ to read about the antibullying laws in your state. Go further and call the nonemergency number for your local police department to speak to an officer assigned to juveniles. Ask the officer to come to your home to talk to you and your child about bullying. Frequently when a child hears a police officer tell him what could happen, he pays attention and tries to correct his ways before someone presses charges against him.

If your child persists in bullying, ask your family doctor for a referral to a child psychologist. Usually before a referral is made to a specialist, the doctor conducts a thorough physical examination to ascertain whether there is a medical cause for the abnormal behavior. Make and keep all appointments. You are fighting for your child's health and future.

Children also need to hear that a bad reputation is easy to acquire and difficult to lose, while a good reputation is difficult to acquire but easy to lose. He does not want an ugly reputation to follow him into adulthood.

Bullying among girls can be quite different from that of boys. Girls' bullying is often emotional. Ostracism, heckling, taunting, teasing, and belittling are some of the "mean" behaviors in which girls engage. The damage can be just as great as physical violence. Take the matter up with the teacher, and do not be afraid to ask her to have a conference with the parents of the bullies. Tell your daughter to make it clear to the girls that she does not and will not seek their friendship; avoid the girls; and let you know if they approach her again. If they do approach your daughter after you have told her to avoid them and she has, it is time to consult the principal.

Insist that these girls' behavior toward your daughter be handled as bullying and a threat to her well-being.

Bullying among siblings is also a problem. Follow the advice given above to stop such bullying immediately.

88. Deliberately schedule quality time with your child, especially if you are busy.

Quality time is a time for bonding, which is extremely important for the interpersonal relationship between parent and child and for healthy emotional development. Bonding builds trust as well as a sense of safety and security that all children need. Children must be able to trust that parents will meet their physical, emotional, and social needs. Talk to infants; play with toddlers and preschoolers; encourage grade-schoolers and give them sound advice about life, morality, human behavior, responsibility, and education; arm middle- and high schoolers with information and guidance about the changes in their bodies, interactions with the opposite gender, occupational and vocational opportunities, responsibilities, and independence. Remember, it takes very little to please a child, and the regularity of this kind of activity can help children find comfort and stability.

One idea for quality time is to create a family tradition every Friday, Saturday, or Sunday that your child will remember, talk, and laugh about in his adult years. The special event can revolve around a special meal, activity, or location in which conversation and laughter are abundant. Possibilities include the following:

- Saturday night pizza and lemonade
- weekly baseball games
- a weekly or biweekly walk around the neighborhood
- a monthly trip to a favorite restaurant

- a bimonthly trip to the movies
- an annual treat to an at-home or away professional ballgame with all the trimmings

Many occupations require workers to attend an annual conference, retreat, or training session. Consider taking your child with you specifically to bond. If you can, share and discuss the workshops you are attending. Research, share, and discuss your findings about the history, architecture, dialects, and culture of the conference's locale. Don't forget to look into guided and unguided tours sponsored by the conference hosts or the conference city, often free of charge.

Ask if the hotel in which you will be staying has a sitting service. Coworkers may be willing to pool their money to pay for licensed sitters to constructively engage the children while you attend to business, or you might hire a sitter to travel with you so you and your spouse can supervise the children's educational activities and have some alone time. Conference sessions usually run from eight in the morning to five in the evening, but there is usually time for at least one bonding activity per day with your children.

Bonding activities provide not only fun times but also good, long-lasting memories—memories that later on in life your children can share with each other and with their own children.

89. Periodically ask your child how he feels about his day.

"How did your day go?" is the usual question asked by a parent. "Okay" or "I played and ate lunch" are the typical responses. To get more details, try prodding with humor: "You had lunch *all day?*" or "How many hours did you spend in the gym?" Think out loud so he can hear that you plan to schedule a teacher conference to find out why lunch and playground are the only activities. This may spur him to be more forthcoming.

If getting a response is like pulling teeth, ask whether his day was productive or boring; whether there was a high point or a low point; whether something happened to make him happy, satisfied, angry, sad, or indifferent. Ask him to tell you about the topics discussed in specific classes: reading, literature, math, science, social studies, geography. Ask what he overheard in the hallways before, during, after, and between classes. Ask to see his notes in each subject and to explain them to you. Ask about the day's lessons.

Do not be surprised if your child cannot read his notes or explain the concepts or processes. His unclear, illegible, disorganized, or incomplete notes may be posing a problem—and creating an emotional response—when it comes to doing homework, reviewing, or studying for a quiz or test. If notes are chaotic, ask for one of his textbooks and then silently read a section or chapter. Next, have him read silently what you read. Follow up with questions about what the both of you have read. His answers may confirm or reject the possibility of literacy problems. If such problems are suspected, ask his teachers to provide alternative reading materials and provide literacy tutoring.

If your child does not bring home his textbooks, tell him to do so. If he is not allowed to bring textbooks home, write a note asking the teacher to let him bring them home. If she declines or ignores the request, call to speak to the assistant principal or principal and explain that he needs them to study the explanations, examples, and illustrations to verify the accuracy of his notes and to do additional reading in preparation for quizzes and tests. If there is no positive response, ask whether the school has a tutoring or after-school program in which children may use the library to access the textbooks. A copy of each textbook should be available in the school's library. If not, request in writing to have these books placed in the library. Your child has a right to those books because your taxpayer dollars helped to purchase them.

Your inquiry into his feelings about his day may result in some pretty interesting conversations covering both academic and nonacademic topics, each of which may be positively or negatively fueling his emotions.

90. Nurture your child's unique strengths, abilities, and interests.

Not all children learn alike or have the same interests or skills. Some children have a one-of-a-kind but hidden capability. Parents are in a better position than teachers to identify the strengths, abilities, and interests unique to each child.

Some parents assume the responsibility for developing uniqueness when recognized. For example, a five-year-old struggling to sound out English words astonished his teachers when he insisted he put a car together by "reading the directions." How could this be when, according to their assessment, he could not read? He must have been "reading" the pictures, right? When the boy's teacher approached the mom about the youngster's literacy difficulties, the mom shared that her son did not have any learning problems and explained how she knew: the directions were written in Japanese, which he could not only speak but also read and write. Had she not explained, the teacher may have recommended his placement in a program that could have damaged his self-confidence and self-image or slowed his intellectual development. His parents were happy to inform the staff of their son's abilities they identified, nurtured, and celebrated.

There is a Middle Eastern saying, "One is given more than the other." The adage does not necessarily imply the existence of a hierarchy in which one is greater, superior, or better than the other—a probable misinterpretation. It is true each has been given something in a greater or lesser quantity than others. The differing degrees and varieties of strengths, abilities, and interests complement each other, hopefully creating a harmonious, highly productive society.

Likewise, every child has been given more of something than others. Although schools attempt to find what that "more" is by offering an array of liberal arts and vocational courses, some children's gifts or interests are still not going to be uncovered. Hence, many teachers are unable to recognize an interest a child may have. Even if they do, they may not know how to nurture it.

For example, an eleven-year-old inherited an interest in physics from his grandfather, who shared with him many physics ideas and concepts. One day, the youngster was looking out the window, so his teacher asked what he was admiring. His reply was that he was not looking at anything in particular but was thinking about Bernoulli's principle. The teacher remarked, "What is that?" in such a way that his classmates broke into laughter, embarrassing the youngster, who did not want to return to school because he had been mocked and humiliated one too many times. Had the teacher studied physics, she may have recognized the term and advanced the class's knowledge about a concept that helps explain the motion of gas and liquids through narrow conduits or tubes—as in trees and blood vessels. Children with unique gifts need protection from those who do not understand yet choose to belittle.

Beyond nurturing a child's interests, a parent can often find ways to show a student how things learned in school can be related to his interests. For example, most sports involve using math to calculate statistics, such as field-goal percentage in basketball. Often these associations aren't obvious to children.

Parents who realize their children have a unique interest should seek free university- or community-based weekend or summer programs geared to exciting young ones with sciences, mathematics, and humanities. Many parents encourage participation in related but specialized programs and find books for their children to read. Added bonuses are association and interaction with other children who share your child's unique interests. All these activities can nurture and strengthen a child's confidence to appreciate and celebrate his uniqueness and all the joy it promises to bring.

91. Speak positively about your child's teacher or school when your child is present.

If you are upset with the teacher or school, say nothing negative in the presence of your child. He should not be put in a position to be concerned about the teacher or the quality of his instruction—a situation over which he has no control.

When a child hears a parent's negative comments about a teacher or school, he may begin to disrespect, disregard, or reject the teacher and what she offers, resulting in more problems for the child. Instead, request a conference with the teacher to discuss your concerns. Take examples of your child's work to support your argument. Ask how you can help your child as well as how you can help the teacher help your child. Ask the teacher if your child needs a tutor and if so, will she work with the tutor by sharing the areas in which your child needs the most help? Do not depend upon the teacher contacting the tutor; you may need your tutor to contact the teacher. Some teachers resent it when a parent gets a tutor, and in that case there will probably be no communication.

The article "Establishing a Parent-Teacher Relationship" from the Child Development Institute (http://childdevelopmentinfo.com/learning/parent_teacher/) offers some useful information, and its opening statement is quite true: the first meeting is very important, similar to the old saying, "the first impression is a lasting impression."

92. Be on the same page with your child's other parent.

Boys and girls need positive, supportive, consistent, and composed mothers *and* fathers committed to working together toward dynamic parent-child interactions, even when separated or divorced. Parents are urged to discuss and decide how they—together—will handle their children's education, including and especially when the academic performance is poor. Marital frustrations and animosities must not be allowed to impact the children's physical, social, economic, emotional, and academic well-being. Even when parents are at odds, children continue to need consistent, composed, and committed parents capable of setting aside any differences to focus on them.

As parents attempt to work together, they should also take into consideration the possibility that their children may attempt to undermine their cohesion. From birth, children study their parents to learn how to get what they think they need. Some ways to get attention include crying louder and louder and turning blue from holding their breath. Manipulation is learned and is normal.

Older children may resort to unexpected manipulation strategies, such as pitting one parent against the other; misbehaving in school or in the neighborhood; playing on the mother's emotions; or lying and stealing. An extreme manipulation strategy is a diabetic child refusing to measure sugar levels and administer the required insulin bolus even after being hospitalized on the verge of a diabetic coma, all in an attempt to bring the parents back together.

Manipulation does not make a child evil or bad; it is merely a way of "correcting" what he perceives to be wrong. It is the child's way of dealing with stress, which many parents themselves have difficulty doing. Be aware that children newly experiencing their parents' separation or divorce may be coached on manipulation by children whose parents are already separated or divorced.

To prevent manipulation and reduce stress on both parents and children, never speak negatively about the other parent in your child's presence. You may cause the child to do the opposite of what you expected. Ideally, parents should be in agreement about academic, behavioral, and social expectations for their child, as well as limits and the consequences of violating those limits. They should agree to disagree when and where their children cannot possibly hear. Parental composure and consistency reduce stress, increase effectiveness and efficiency for both parents and children, and demonstrate to the children that the parents still care for and are committed to them.

Many times, the parent who is angry with the ex-spouse refuses to allow the other parent to discipline, spend time with, or even talk to the child. The children's academics will probably suffer as a result, and the emotional, stressed parent will begin to threaten and punish. Eventually, out of frustration with downward spiraling grades, the parent may take heed and allow the other parent to be actively involved.

It makes sense to call the other parent to explain what is happening with the children. The other parent's response may include making a visit to the school, showing up for parent-teacher conferences, calling teachers to provide a contact phone number, taking the children out, and/or laying down or reinforcing the rules and implementing the consequences when the rules are broken. A testy divorce may turn amiable, and the children's academic performance may soar. It has happened.

Parents must never use the children as a weapon against the other parent, and both parents should be informed and have input about the academic progress of each child. Two calm heads are needed to discuss and then decide together how the children's education, especially poor academic performance, will be handled. Outcomes and expectations may be agreed upon, including when, where, and how to study as well as ways a parent's absence may be felt, especially by the son in the father's absence.

At some point, many boys decide to ignore their mother's directions. When the son repeatedly disobeys the mother's requests, it may be the son's way of calling for his father's or a significant male figure's attention. It is also the mother's cue to allow Dad to step in. Often, as the male child gets older, he becomes much more difficult for the mother to handle. She should realize this and prepare for it at the beginning of the split by not obstructing the father's involvement in his son's life.

93. Avoid a pattern of defending or making excuses for your child's missteps.

Defending and protecting your child can go too far, resulting in the creation of a monster whose behaviors escalate from bad to worse. Instead of constantly defending or making excuses, recognize and admit to yourself—and, when appropriate, to others—that your child can and does make mistakes, if for no other reason than that he is human.

Repeat offenses should be dealt with more sternly than those before. When mistakes are costly to the child or to others, the child responsible should be required to pay restitution. Do not let him get away with frequent misbehavior, no matter how good or poor a student he is. Levy consequences that get his attention. Remember, parents whose children have been victimized can, on behalf of their children, call the police, press charges, and sue for damages—especially when the parent of the offending child is unreasonable.

94. Avoid making your child helpless.

If your child repeatedly says, "I don't understand" or "I don't get it," he may be becoming helpless. Helplessness develops over time, often with the assistance of parents and in some instances grandparents. If you can find it, watch *The Pinks and the Blues*, a PBS video first aired in 1960 and again in 1974. It shows how parents unwittingly create helplessness in a child, especially a female child, through culturally learned and transmitted body language, speech, and expectations. Another useful resource on stereotyping and helplessness is "Sex Stereotyping" on the PsychAlive website (http://www.psychalive.org/sexual-stereotyping/).

Parents send a subliminal message to the child when they sit by his side "coaching" or suggesting answers for his homework. The message is that the child lacks the ability to do the work alone. Consider weaning your child from your assistance. Expect him to react to your change in behavior. You may hate hearing his whining or crying, but the habit of his relying on you to make the grade must be broken. Independently of you or an older sibling, he must learn to write his papers and speeches, do his projects, complete and check his own work—because he is capable of doing it. When the urge to help descends, remind yourself that you cannot take his tests or accompany him to an interview. He has to grow up and be able to fend for himself. It is better for him to fall down now when he is young than later when he is in high school.

It is all too easy for your help to become a harm. Gradually, your child will lose his self-confidence and doubts his own abilities. A must-watch video is "Learned Helplessness" on YouTube at https://www.youtube.com/watch?v=gFmFOmprTt0. Khan Academy Health and Medicine hosts two more YouTube videos related to learned helplessness: "Personal Control (Locus of Control,

Learned Helplessness, and the Tyranny of Choice)" at https://www.youtube.com/watch?v=Vx1dnPMPhl0 and "Self Esteem, Self Efficacy, and Locus of Control" at https://www.youtube.com/watch?v=xcLKlPTG97k.

Ask yourself if you do any of the following for your child:

- clean out his book bag to make it neat
- label his notebooks or regularly put paper in his binder
- clean his room or pick up his clothes
- complete his chores instead of insisting he finish the task correctly
- make his lunch and/or lay out his clothes daily after age nine
- get him up for school after giving him an alarm clock
- help with his assignments when he cries or whines that he needs your assistance
- sit by his side or help him with his assignments every night
- often complete his spoken sentences
- give him answers, even when he does not ask for them
- complete his assignments

Children are capable of doing a lot of things for themselves, one of which is achieving academic excellence. The more parents do these things for them, the more dependent and helpless they become. Stop being afraid for your child; it is natural for a child to fall, stumble, and make mistakes. In fact, mistakes are the way children learn and prepare for adulthood. It is better for him to stumble when younger than when older.

95. Protect your child's self-confidence and self-respect.

Once a child's self confidence or self-respect has been shaken, restoring it is extremely difficult. He may experience success in one instance and then doubt himself immediately afterward. Years later, he may still need continual reminders that he can and will accomplish. Despite the stubbornness of the shaken self-confidence, the following actions may help:

- Take videos and pictures of his successes and show them to family and friends.
- Praise and encourage him when due.
- Enroll him in activities that add to his strengths, talents, and skills, such as swimming, golf, and chess.
- Create and provide opportunities—such as team or individual social events (sport, debate, recitation)—where he earns your praise and the praise of others.
- Encourage him to do something unique that will yield satisfaction and a sense of accomplishment, such as starting a business. Yes, children can start businesses.
- Enter him into academics-related competitions in which he has a good chance of winning or placing. (See #23 and #40 in chapter 4.)
- Enter him into an unusual individual sport. For a list of possibilities, visit the Wikipedia page on individual sports at http://en.wikipedia.org/wiki/Category:Individual_sports.

For additional information, consult *Helping Children with Emotional Problems* by Edward E. Moody Jr., *Managing Children with Problems* by Ved P. Varma, and *Growing up with Divorce: Helping Your Child Avoid Immediate and Later Emotional Problems* by Neil Kalter.[40]

96. Engage in activities that earn and maintain your child's respect.

In both public and private, parents should always model—in action and speech—how they would like their children to behave. When out and about, parents must think about how their children would feel if parental misbehaviors like fighting, arguing, drinking, or creating a scene were to get back to them.

Although children tend to love and respect their parents regardless of embarrassing scenes, they admire adults who help and praise them and who receive positive recognition from others. You can earn and maintain your child's respect by doing one or more of the following:

- behaving inside the home as you would want your child to behave outside the home
- helping to resolve family conflicts
- controlling your anger
- helping a non–family member
- explaining to your child why you help others, including strangers
- keeping bragging or reminiscing about the "good old days" to a minimum
- excelling in an activity

Model how to handle awkward situations. For example, if your child asks about a neighbor or an adult whose behavior or language is embarrassing, explain to your child that something may have happened in that person's childhood to cause her to act and speak the way she does, or that the individual may be ill and cannot help herself. Realistically, one does not know all that a person is going through, and so we should not pass judgment. Tell your child not to speak to this individual's children about her misbehaviors; instead, listen and speak words of comfort. Explain that her children probably are embarrassed, feel uncomfortable, and do not need additional stress. It is better to be a good listener than a giver of advice, especially when inexperienced in human behavior.

97. Teach your child to be responsible.

Responsibility relates to many things in life, such as organization, trustworthiness, confidence, courage, and independence. Teaching responsibility can be a difficult task. Stubborn and strong-willed children will test your mettle. Be prepared to win, because many children think of work, including academic work, in terms of money and reward. Rarely do they recognize the role work plays in building character. Yet work is vital to your child's education, and succeeding will give him confidence in the future.

Start off by giving your child one or more daily chores for which he alone is responsible. It may be as simple as making the bed, cleaning the bathroom, and mopping the kitchen floor. Increase the responsibility load to two or three tasks that take place one or two days a week, such as doing the laundry, taking out the trash, bringing in and cleaning the garbage cans, weeding or mowing the lawn, and cleaning out and washing the car. Ensure the task has been done well; if it is not, have your child redo or make the corrections, and then offer your praise.

For your middle and high school child, try "Jump$tart's Reality Check" at http://www.jumpstart.org/reality-check.html to get him thinking about what he wants and will need to maintain himself in the future. Follow up with a discussion about what he needs to do to achieve his goals. Of course, education will be in the mix; however, make sure his responsibility for himself is included, for he must learn independence, which assumes responsibility. Make it clear you will not call, write, or visit to remind him of his responsibilities.

98. Praise and commend your child for improving or doing well in school.

Many parents directly praise their child by saying, "You did a good job!" or giving tangible rewards for work done well. However, indirect praise and attention also motivate children to continue learning and achieving. Examples of indirect praise are his overhearing you telling a friend, neighbor, or family member how well he is doing, or receiving a phone call from Grandma and Grandpa commending him for his successful completion of a major assignment. When talking to a sibling, give your child credit for using specific strategies to accomplish a task. Do not forget to announce academic achievements at family reunions, Sunday school, or wherever children are being recognized. Do not overdo it, though; you may put unnecessary pressure on your child.

99. Use role-play to show your child how to handle difficult personalities and incidents at school.

Before your child experiences conflict, discuss the possibility and what he might do to avoid or diffuse the situation. Role-play to show him how to use communication skills to avoid and resolve teasing, harassment, mockery, wrongdoing, and fighting. In your role-play, include strategies like using humor and calm, reasoned speech while edging toward an exit or safety from the antagonist. If the threat is violent, stress that when backing up, your child must not take his eyes off the attacker. Include what to do immediately after the incident. Role-play reporting the incident to the police or the principal and then to you.

In your role-play, include what you will do upon hearing about the incident. Remember to chose your words well and to be calm; many children avoid telling their parents about conflicts out of fear of what the parent will do. They assume your actions will make matters worse for them. Role-playing may be a good exercise for you too. Consider practicing in the mirror before practicing with your child.

Many storybooks for young children illustrate how to resolve a conflict. For older children, however, sources addressing the more serious and realistic situations seem to diminish in number. Do a web search for "confessions of bullies" to see several sites where bullies have shared how they stopped terrorizing others. These sites suggest ways to deal with frightening, humiliating, and hurtful digs and threats to your child.

Although *martial* means warfare, even in martial arts instruction, avoidance of conflict is paramount. Douglas Orr, owner of the Scholar Warrior Institute Kuk Sul Hapkido in Greensboro, North Carolina, says, "Many of today's martial arts are 'sport oriented,' but traditional martial arts classes in addition to self-defense focus on communication techniques to avoid physical confrontation; role playing is used to effectively accomplish the task." You may wish to consult someone in martial arts in your area for role-playing suggestions. You may also visit "Preventing Conflict—How to Avoid Conflict?" on the Management Study Guide site at http://managementstudyguide.com/preventing-conflict.htm for more ideas on role-playing with older children.

100. Guide your child in selecting appropriate friends and activities.

An important aspect of social development that takes place throughout your child's school years is learning how to select friends and activities. Before high school graduation, your child must be able to control his environment to minimize interference with his studies, classes, and work. Selecting friends who are supportive and activities for relaxation and academic enhancement is an important decision for the teenager and young adult to make. Each distraction has its lure, but your child must begin to learn, preferably during elementary school, how to select for himself the best friends and activities not only for his social and emotional development but also for his academic, professional, and economic advancement.

Encourage your child to think not only of the immediate but also of the future consequences of his choices. For example, friends who steal, disrespect their parents, sneak out of the house, or drink every weekend are not really friends. Friends are people he can have fun with, depend upon, and trust to tell him the truth about himself. Your child may assume he will have his current buddies for life. Explain that the older he gets, the less interaction he will have with his current friends. After graduation, friends find themselves going separate ways: school, employment, military. Do not forget to mention that although true friendship can last a lifetime, most people have few friends.

When a child asks advice about helping a friend in need, ask if he has the strength, skills, or resources to adequately help his friend. His response is likely to be no. Children, adolescents, and college students are usually ill equipped to help anyone with bad habits or thoughts; they lack sufficient time and skills needed to genuinely help. As a friend, your child can do more by stating that he will no longer be friends with this individual if the misbehavior persists and then suggesting that his friend seek help. Tell your child if his friends successfully draw him into their mischief, his immediate and future plans may be delayed or destroyed. Your child should consider whether he wants this person and this person's problems in his life for a lifetime.

Engaging in too many activities also interferes with academic goals, for the same reason: insufficient time to properly execute responsibilities. Advise your child to limit his choices to two, no more than three. Consider whether he has adequate time to perform well in all of his academic and nonacademic responsibilities. If the answer is no or maybe, he should eliminate or reduce the number of activities. Discuss with your child how to make sound choices from among the many, many existing ones. In so doing, you are preparing him for the upper grades, college, adulthood, and life.

101. Find ways to help your child strengthen social interactions.

Most parents teach basic manners, such as saying "thank you," "no thank you," "you are welcome," "excuse me," "forgive me," and "please." As your child matures, he needs socially acceptable, appropriate, interpersonal written and spoken communication skills for a variety of informal and formal settings, including school, the public, social media, interviews, and negotiations. Role-playing and etiquette lessons are two ways to strengthen your child's ability to avoid rudeness, ridicule, and embarrassment.

In a fun way, role-playing teaches, rehearses, and strengthens your child's manners. If you need to brush up on a few niceties, visit "Handling Introductions Properly" on the Family Education site at http://life.familyeducation.com/making-introductions/etiquette/48930.html. For role playing ideas and gifts, consider the following books:

- for preschoolers, *The Pigeon Needs a Bath!* by Mo Willems
- for preteens and teens, *How Rude! The Teen Guide to Good Manners, Proper Behavior, and Not Grossing People Out* by Alex J. Packer
- for the college bound, *Getting Ahead with Etiquette: Roadmap to Success for Young Adults, Teens, and College Students* by Tina Hayes[41]

Another useful resource is "40 Etiquette Tips" on the Business Training Works site at http://www.businesstrainingworks.com/training-resources/40-workplace-etiquette-tips.

Free or low-cost classes may be offered by a variety of community-based organizations, including the local chamber of commerce, a nonprofit organization promoting good will, or a religious community engaged in international work. If the classes are difficult to find, ask a university international program director for suggestions.

Some children feel a need to participate in risky or risqué activities in order to make and keep friends. Consider getting a community organization to offer preteen and teen workshops addressing, for example, social media etiquette, which skillfully weaves in the legalities and dangers of inappropriate language and behaviors like cyberbullying and sexting. Of course, excelling in an academic or nonacademic activity enhances your child's social standing among his peers, enabling him to feel emotionally secure in both academic and nonacademic settings.

102. Never compare one child to another.

Comparing one child to another can have lifelong effects. Each child is different, and children's experiences and interpretations of life events are and will be different—even among identical twins. Although you may perceive their degree of difference to be slight, their experiences and interpretations of those experiences will remain different. Expect their academic, social, physical, and emotional behaviors to be different as well.

Statements like "Your brother gets straight As. Why don't you?" should never be made, because such comparisons evoke hostility and resentment and deny both children's individualities. Indirect suggestions, such as "Your brother did such and such, do you think it may work for you?" are a step in the right direction, but it is best to make the recommendation without mentioning the sibling.

103. Discuss with your child elements in television programming, advertisements, and social media that demean authority figures.

Children, especially young ones who have difficulty separating fact from opinion and reality from fiction, need balanced exposure to productive, intelligent, diverse characters. Unfortunately, children's TV shows often portray parents, teachers, and ethnic group members as airheads. Particularly irritating are portrayals of fathers as less intelligent than other family members.

Studies continue to indicate that children in the United States spend an extraordinary number of hours—twenty-eight to thirty-two per week—watching television.[42] In addition to restricting the number of hours your child watches, you may wish to discuss with your child whether specific characters on television and the Internet reflect reality, bigotry, propaganda, or stereotypes—including racism, sexism, classism, and elitism. Another topic to discuss is whether the characters shape children's thoughts about their parents or entire groups of people.

Social media is another animal. One parent was overheard saying to another parent . . . "It erodes the trust I thought I had with my child ... I simply cannot trust." *Erode* is the perfect word, because social media eats up time and breaks down parental authority. The effects can be devastating and include poor grades, sneaking, lying, defiance, and deceit.

104. Send consistent messages to your child about his education.

When a parent wonders why her child is performing poorly academically, she should look first at herself. Has she been constantly checking homework or notebooks, repeatedly levying consequences for missed deadlines, regularly applying house rules related to academics, and steadily enforcing the specific time set aside for homework and only homework? Fluctuations in these types of communication between parent, child, and other significant adults are called *mixed messages*, and they can lead to poor academic performance.

Children do not think like adults. To a child, adult inconsistency means the adult either does not care whether he does or does not do his schoolwork or that it is unimportant. A child's invalid assumption about one thing may spill into other areas, such as behavior, organization, or timeliness. Even the best-behaved child may try to escape from doing what is expected.

105. Embolden your child to be assertive.

Assertiveness is demonstrated when taking action and when speaking. It communicates confidence and purpose. If your child seems consistently shy within his comfort zones, such as home or a small group of close friends, encourage him to share his opinions or talk about a subject with which he is quite familiar. As he gains confidence in doing so, suggest he share his thoughts or activities with a wider audience, like classmates.

Next, assign simple tasks requiring a bit more courage—for example, questioning a store clerk or manager about a product before making a purchase. Organizing a neighborhood pet, talent, or art show offers another opportunity to share his thoughts and experiences. An older child can try handling his dog in an American Kennel Club (AKC) sponsored show, which can be tough to do in front of dozens of people and a judge or judges who at times focus solely on him and his pet. If there are no events for children, competing against professional handlers will move him closer to being assertive.

Being assertive enables your child to comfortably take the lead in a variety of settings, such as volunteering to do a job no one else seems to want, making an unusual but sound suggestion, discussing his research on a controversial topic. Stepping out of his comfort zone takes courage, to be sure, so commend and appreciate your child for his bravery. "Assertive, Nonassertive, and Aggressive Behaviors" on the website of the College of New Jersey at http://oavi.tcnj.edu/tools-for-everyone/assertiveness/asscrtive-nonassertive-and-aggressive-behaviors/ offers suggestions of times when nonassertiveness and aggression are useful.

106. Boost your child's ethnic and cultural pride.

To build children's self-confidence, self-respect, and pride, share your extended family's cultural and historical events, personalities, and contributions to the community, city, state, nation, or world. Families possess thousands of untold stories that are hidden from the public, and these will remain forever unknown unless family members make sure they are told, at least to their children.

Knowledge of the family's contributions gives a child confidence that he too can achieve and contribute.

107. Encourage your child to become fluent in one or more foreign languages.

For some time, leaders of this nation have recognized that the educational system has serious faults, one of which is failure to favorably present diverse groups. Curriculum and teacher responses tend to exalt everything mainstream, as if those outside of the mainstream are insignificant. Gross ignorance of and indifference to others is not a good practice when the classroom, school, city, state, and country are politically, economically, and inextricably dependent on those inside and outside of its borders.

Learning to speak a different language opens a child's eyes and mind to the different ways people view life, nature, and the world around them. For example, children of different cultures are perceived as having reached adulthood at different times and in different ways. Foreign-language learning facilitates the realization that diversity is nothing to fear.

Consider also that learning to speak, read, and write a foreign language may open doors for your adult child to earn a bonus or land employment in a highly competitive, well-paying arena like international business, medicine, technology, or corporate law. The younger a child is when learning a foreign language, the more competent he will be.[43]

On top of all of this, there is, according to Martha G. Abbott, director of education for the American Council on the Teaching of Foreign Languages, "research … that shows that children who study a foreign language, even when this second language study takes away from the study of mathematics, outperform (on standardized tests of mathematics) students who do not study a foreign language and have more mathematical instruction during the school day. Again, this research upholds the notion that learning a second language is an exercise in cognitive problem solving and that the effects of second language instruction are directly transferable to the area of mathematical skill development."[44]

108. Arm your child with tales and sayings that offer guidance in school and life.

Throughout human history, parents have equipped their children with fables, tales, and sayings to teach appropriate behaviors, attitudes, and knowledge. The following are sample tales, fables, and sayings appropriate for children of all ages:

- Old tales
  - "The Man, the Boy, and the Donkey"
    Lesson—do not listen to those who do not know your circumstances.
  - "The Boy Who Cried Wolf"
    Lessons—call for help only when help is needed; telling the truth maintains one's reputation of integrity.
  - "Buridan's Donkey"
    Lesson—indecision can result in death or the loss of an opportunity, a goal, or the realization of a dream. For a mental and philosophical exercise relating this tale to human free will, see *Finitude: A Study of Cognitive Limits and Limitations* by Nicholas Rescher.

- Classic Aesop
  - "The Ant and the Grasshopper"
    Lesson—prepare now for tomorrow.
  - "The Tortoise and the Hare"
    Lessons—do not become overly confident; slow and methodical can meet the challenge.

- o "The Goose that Laid the Golden Egg"
  Lesson—patience is a virtue, impatience is folly.

- Maxims
  - o "Tomorrow always comes."
    Lesson—time cannot be stopped, so be prepared for the inevitable.
  - o "Cleanliness is next to godliness."
    Lesson—groom before visiting and praying in God's house.
  - o "Don't judge a book by its cover."
    Lesson—appearances can be deceiving.
  - o "Beauty is skin-deep; ugly, to the bone."
    Lesson—one's personality must also be pleasing.
  - o "If at first you don't succeed, try, try again."
    Lesson—don't give up easily.
  - o "Haste makes waste."
    Lesson—hurrying can result in a loss of time.
  - o "The first impression is a lasting impression."
    Lesson—for that first encounter, dress to impress.

- Benjamin Franklin's *Poor Richard's Almanac*
  - o "A stitch in time saves nine."
    Lesson—act at the first sign of trouble.
  - o "An ounce of prevention is worth a pound of cure."
    Lesson—use observation and information to ward off potential/possible trouble; be proactive, not reactive.
  - o "Never leave till tomorrow what can be done today."
    Lesson—do not procrastinate!

- Stories/Plays
  - o *Why Mosquitoes Buzz in People's Ears*

Lesson—assumptions are dangerous, so verify your thoughts and feelings before acting.

109. Have your energetic, overactive child exercise for twenty to thirty minutes every morning before going to school.

Exercise burns excess energy that will interfere with your child's ability to focus in class. Outdoor exercise—such as jogging, walking, jumping rope, and swimming—is an excellent morning energy burner. Additionally, your child gets his daily dose of vitamin D (from sunshine) needed to avoid softening of the bones. On rainy days, indoor exercise can include jumping rope, using the treadmill, or engaging in aerobics.

110. Dispute your preteen's or teenager's belief that an education is out of reach.

Your child is going to need a lot of tender loving care, and you are going to need a lot of patience, because a child at this stage is truly emotionally upset. His self-image and self-confidence probably have been dashed. You must do many things at once: create opportunities for success, carefully introduce success in academics, increase depth and breadth of academic learning to bring him up to level, and then accelerate his studies. Wow! How do you do this?

If, when pressed about educational performance, your child has angry or violent outbursts, he is actually expressing his pain from frustration, hurt, shame, disappointment, and embarrassment. Tell him you want to help and that when he is ready to talk, you will listen. When that time comes, tell him again that you really want to help and are willing to listen. Be sure to listen without saying one word.

Your listening may be painful, because you will probably be blamed for everything or at least for playing a part in his failures. Frankly, for him to have reached this level of frustration, you probably did play a part. Do not try to justify or explain your actions or words. Listen! Utter not one word until he has finished.

When he finishes, apologize, several times if you feel the need to. Then ask him how and what the two of you can do together to accomplish his goals—get help with school, build friendships, rid him of his anger, restore his self-confidence, whatever he perceives to be the root of his problem. He may respond that he has no idea what to do or he may respond with anger, again rejecting your help. Do not push. Tell him you will come up with a plan soon and that you will share it with him to see if he approves and is willing to let you work with him on it. Notice you are encouraging him to take the decision-making lead. Do not be surprised if he asks you to take the lead.

Chances are your child has a serious reading problem that was not caught earlier. Get professional help from a reading specialist, or contact a local university to find a graduate student majoring in literacy who can assess his literacy skills and perhaps provide some tutoring. Most if not all literacy teacher training programs require students to work with children with severe reading problems. Also ask a nearby college or community college if it sponsors a tutoring program for school-age children. Call social services to find out if they have both a free or low-cost mediation program and a literacy program. A mediator may be able to help you and your child resolve a problem without erupting into an argument.

Even when your child's actions seem beyond repair, you must never give up. Consult a family counselor for ways to repair your broken parent-child relationship. You may be your child's only hope. Family services are usually free or low cost under certain circumstances. Do not be embarrassed; these counselors have heard worse.

111. Use consequences that involve research and learning to change stubborn, unacceptable behaviors.

By definition, *research* is the search for and uncovering of facts that expand and/or change a body of knowledge, learning, and/or behavior. Bibliotherapy, the use of reading material to help someone deal with emotions, may help your child find appropriate and acceptable ways to handle negative emotional feelings. For example, a thirteen-year-old who repeatedly calls male classmates "gay" when he feels a need to insult them might be assigned a five-page essay to explain why his language is harmful not only to the targeted victim but also to himself. The essay must include quotations and references to real-life events and court cases. After finishing the essay, he must write and send a grammatically correct apology to each of his victims. Finally, he must share his findings and his apology with the class.

This practical and instructive assignment, requiring the application of reading, writing, and reflection, was actually made under the circumstances described. Through the articles and court cases, the student learned that at least three children repeatedly called "gay" committed suicide, which made him realize his words could have caused one of his classmates to take his life and that the child's death would have haunted him for the rest of his life. The written apology was movingly sincere, but more importantly the experience helped him break his abusive habit. The American Library Association website contains useful information about bibliotherapy (ala.org/tools/bibliotherapy). For a list of books on topics disconcerting to children, visit the following links:

- "Bibliotherapy and Realistic Fiction," Library Book Lists, http://librarybooklists.org/fiction/children/jbibliotherapy.htm
- "Children's Books Assist Children in Dealing with Strong Feelings and Tragedy," Michigan State

University Extension, http://msue.anr.msu.edu/
news/childrens_books_assist_children_in_dealing_
with_strong_feelings_and_tragedy

Notes

33 Katherine Kam, "How Anger Can Hurt Your Heart," WebMD, accessed
    April 30, 2015, http://www.webmd.com/balance/stress-management/
    features/how-anger-hurts-your-heart.
34 Carla Amurao, "Fact Sheet: How Bad Is the School to Prison Pipeline?"
    Education Under Arrest, ep. 6, *Tavis Smiley Reports*, PBS.org, accessed
    April 30, 2015, http://www.pbs.org/wnet/tavissmiley/tsr/education-
    under-arrest/school-to-prison-pipeline-fact-sheet/; "School-to-Prison
    Pipeline," American Civil Liberties Union, accessed April 30, 2015,
    https://www.aclu.org/school-prison-pipeline; "School to Prison Pipeline,"
    NAACP Legal Defense and Education Fund, accessed April 30, 2015,
    http://www.naacpldf.org/case/school-prison-pipeline (note: this site
    provides a somewhat updated list of legal cases related to education/
    schools).
35 Laura Biel, "Emotional Wounds," *Science News* 186, no. 12 (December
    13, 2014): 22–25; Cara J. Kiff, Liliana J. Lengua, and Maureen
    Zalewski, "Nature and Nurturing: Parenting in the Context of Child
    Temperament," *Clinical Child and Family Psychology Review* 14, no. 3
    (September 2011): 251–301, http://www.ncbi.nlm.nih.gov/pmc/articles/
    PMC3163750/.
36 "Children's Rights: International and National Laws and Practices,"
    Library of Congress, accessed May 2, 2015, http://www.loc.gov/law/help/
    child-rights/.
37 Kathryn Baer, "Homeless DC Parents Fear Loss of Children ... and
    They're Right," *Poverty & Policy*, May 21, 2012, https://povertyandpolicy.
    wordpress.com/2012/05/21/homeless-dc-parents-fear-loss-of-children-
    and-theyre-right/; Homelessness Resource Center, accessed April 30,
    2015, http://homeless.samhsa.gov/Search.aspx?search=Child Abuse
    and Neglect&journal=Child Abuse and Neglect; "State to Provide
    Homeless Children with Equal Access to Public Education," August
    12, 2008, American Civil Liberties Union, https://www.aclu.org/
    racial-justice_prisoners-rights_drug-law-reform_immigrants-rights/
    state-provide-homeless-children-eq.

38   Ed Mazza, "Second-Grade Bully Cameron Thompson Changes His Ways, Starts Club to Fight Bullying (VIDEO)," *Huffington Post*, May 27, 2014, http://www.huffingtonpost.com/2014/05/27/cameron-thompson-bully-club_n_5395664.html.

39   "How Does Bullying Affect Health and Well-Being?" National Institutes of Health, accessed January 22, 2016, https://www.nichd.nih.gov/health/topics/bullying/conditioninfo/Pages/health.aspx.

40   Edward E. Moody Jr., *Helping Children with Emotional Problems* (Nashville: Randall House Publications, 2010); Ved P. Varma, *Managing Children with Problems* (London: Cassell, 1996); Neil Kalter, *Growing up with Divorce: Helping Your Child Avoid Immediate and Later Emotional Problems* (New York: Free Press, 1990).

41   Mo Willems, *The Pigeon Needs a Bath!* (New York: Disney-Hyperion, 2015); Alex J. Packer, *How Rude! The Teen Guide to Good Manners, Proper Behavior, and Not Grossing People Out*, rev. ed. (Minneapolis: Free Spirit Publishing, 2014); Tina Hayes, *Getting Ahead with Etiquette: Roadmap to Success for Young Adults, Teens, and College Students* (Oakley, California: Cheemah Publishing, 2013).

42   Kyla Boyse, "Television and Children," University of Michigan Health System, last modified August 2010, http://www.med.umich.edu/yourchild/topics/tv.htm; David Perlmutter, "Brain Development: How Much TV Should Children Watch?" *Huffington Post,* December 5, 2010, http://www.huffingtonpost.com/dr-david-perlmutter-md/television-and-the-develo_b_786934.html.

43   Turgan Dinçay, "Advantages of Learning a Foreign Language at an Early Age," *Today's Zaman*, November 25, 2011, http://www.todayszaman.com/op-ed_advantages-of-learning-a-foreign-language-at-an-early-age_263877.html.

44   Martha G. Abbott, Therese Sullivan Caccavale, and Ken Stewart, "Cognitive Benefits of Learning Language," *Duke Gifted Letter* 8, no. 1 (Fall 2007), http://www.actfl.org/advocacy/discover-languages/for-parents/cognitive.

Chapter 7

PREPARING FOR COLLEGE

Just as preparation for high school begins in the primary grades with learning to read, write, and calculate, preparation for college begins in middle school so that by the ninth grade—freshman year—a child knows exactly what he must do to be admitted to at least one of the colleges of his choice. Preparation may involve more than your child realizes, as you will see in this chapter.

112. Have your middle school child target five colleges to research.

Getting into college is becoming more and more competitive, so your child needs to know what he must accomplish between the ninth and eleventh grades to meet the colleges' admissions requirements. Begin his preparation by having him identify the following three pieces of information for each of five targeted schools (later, perhaps in his sophomore year, expand that to ten): grade-point index, the ranking of the department in which he intends to major, and the admissions criteria.

Grade-point index

Knowing the average high school grade point average (HSGPA) of the two or three most recent incoming freshman classes helps your child identify the grades for which he should be aiming. For example, if your child is interested in a school at which the incoming freshman class has an average HSGPA of 3.5, he must aim for more As than Bs in each of his subjects.

Ranking for the intended major

Your child should want to go to the school that offers him the best program for his major. The Peterson's guide to colleges, available in book form or online (https://www.petersons.com), provides this type of information and much more. Your child may be surprised that many of the "big name" schools he's heard of because of their sports teams do not have the top programs in his major. Often, lesser-known schools are the shining stars. Top-notch programs are squirreled in colleges like Harvey Mudd College in California and the Rose-Hulman Institute of Technology in Indiana— among the nation's top schools for undergraduate engineering and nanotechnology.

Admissions criteria

College criteria usually consist of the following:

- course requirements
- minimum number of high school credit hours, if any
- letters of recommendation
- SAT or ACT requirements.

These pieces of information are needed early so that your child has time to improve study habits, take additional courses during the school year or in summer school, identify at least three potential references, and find ways to pay for the advertised and hidden costs of attending. There is a tool to help you determine whether there is a good match between your child and the college: google "college tracker" and click on the response that includes "prepare & apply." Type in the first few letters of the college name and then click the name of the college as it pops up. It will take you to the page where the average HSGPA by year (class) is listed. This HSGPA may be one of your child's objectives.

113. Discuss with your child what admissions officers seek.

Middle school is not too soon to make your child aware of what he needs to do or have to be admitted to a postsecondary school. An impressive transcript filled with As and Bs certainly helps to reflect the quality of the high school graduate, but other ingredients must also be addressed. Remember the adage "First impressions are lasting impressions," because a college admissions officer's first impression may come from the cover letter of the application or the application itself. All correspondence must contain typed, grammatically correct sentences with clear, logical statements and supporting details—and be to the point. Required handwritten compositions must be neat and legible. Writing skills therefore need attention.

Letters of recommendation add another dimension to the quality of the applicant. Your child should politely ask someone who knows his best qualities and who will write truthful comments with one or two examples that demonstrate his commitment to his intellectual development. The request should be made in person or by phone, and your child should never wait until the last minute to ask for a letter of recommendation. Late requests place undue pressure on the recommender, who needs time to compose the best recommendation. Manners must be practiced at all times.

The ability to speak (in Standard English) and interact appropriately with a stranger are among the key ingredients of a quality applicant. The interview allows the admissions officer or committee to listen to and evaluate the candidate's ability to effectively and assertively express his views in Standard English and to observe his ability to appropriately interact with a person or persons in authority and/or power positions—what colleges want in their applicants. In light of this, remind your child not to schedule any other appointments on the day of the interview, for he has no idea what the interviewer may have planned: possibilities include meeting the dean and faculty; having lunch with students and faculty; and additional interviews with other key personnel (such as the dean of students, fraternity brothers, and alumni). One student was introduced to the custodial staff.

To test how an applicant handles stress, the interviewer may make him wait an hour or more, just to see how he reacts. Even after a long wait, a pleasant and calm introduction and departure with firm handshakes are necessary.

By all means, an applicant should have something to talk about. Often the officer will ask the prospective student to say something about himself. This is where unique hobbies, travels, skills, and adventures can come into play. If the student intends to combine majors, such as engineering and medicine, he can explain why such a combination is exciting to him. Showing excitement about something often turns out to be a particularly effective selling point.

Colleges and universities want well-rounded, personable, intelligent candidates who will represent the institution well during and after their matriculation, because a quality graduate is the best recruitment tool. Ask your child and yourself what he brings to the table. What does he possess that sets him apart from the hundreds of other applicants? Find and emphasize it.

114. Make your high school student aware of the importance of GPA.

In a recent study of approximately eighty thousand students attending a California university, researchers found that

> high school grade point average (HSGPA) is consistently the best predictor not only of freshman grades in college, the outcome indicator most often employed in predictive-validity studies, *but also of four-year college outcomes as well.* (emphasis added)[45]

The quote suggests that an incoming freshman with a HSGPA of 2.0 or 2.5 has a high probability of earning a 2.0 or 2.5 not only during his first year but also over his four years of college. Of course, the outcomes are merely predictions that can be forestalled by greatly improved study habits and/or attitude.

Your middle school child must understand that by the time he reaches ninth grade, he must have good study habits already and sharpen those skills throughout high school, college, and graduate school. Have *him* research the GPAs of incoming freshman classes of his targeted colleges so that he can see for himself what is demanded of him. (Google "college tracker." If the HSGPAs are not posted, call the college's admissions office to ask for them.) Neither you nor your high school senior with a B– average wants to be shocked to find his schools of choice have incoming freshman classes with HSGPAs higher than his. For example, traditional high school students (fifteen to eighteen years old) accepted in the UNC–Chapel Hill incoming class of 2019 class have an average HSGPA of 3.70; Boston University, 3.64; Spelman College, 3.36; Case Western Reserve, 3.75; Howard University, 3.23; Harvard University, 3.84; and Mary Baldwin College, 3.02.[46] Grades matter!

115. Discuss how your child's transcript reveals his attitude toward his studies.

Admissions officers seek students who show the potential to graduate from college with a decent GPA. "Potential" may be reflected by trends in high school grade patterns. For example, grades that steadily increase year to year from low to high strongly suggest diligence, determination, commitment to intellectual development, and improved study habits. A student who wants to be a doctor should have grades of A in most if not all of his science courses. Poor grades in the sciences may indicate a lack of preparation for a rigorous course of study, which premed is. A fluctuating (up and down) grade pattern may signal inconsistent study habits, perhaps because the applicant performs according to the courses or teachers he likes or dislikes—not a sign of maturity.

116. Discuss how your child's GPA may limit his field of study.

In some instances, the list of programs available to students with low HSGPAs shortens because each school (such as arts and sciences) or department (such as chemistry) requires a different GPA for acceptance into the major. Competition for a limited number of slots can be keen, especially when colleges and universities across the state don't offer the same major. For example, not all colleges within a state offer an undergraduate nursing degree. Fewer offer undergraduate engineering majors, and even fewer offer cutting-edge undergraduate majors like biomedical engineering, biotechnology, marine biology, or aerospace studies. Perhaps three universities in the country offer an undergraduate minor in nanoscience or nanotechnology. Parents and students must also realize that among the criteria for the accreditation of college departments is the employment rate of graduates. Admissions officers seek students who have potential for employment success.

Competition for a major may be a factor in admission to a college. Despite businesses demanding high-quality graduates with specific degrees in or related to science, technology, engineering, and mathematics (STEM), each department may have a limited number of students it can admit. Saturated fields are those in which there are more graduates holding the degree than there are employment positions available. Application to a saturated field may impact admissions decisions.

Students with a passion for competitive or saturated fields can make themselves attractive by stating on the application an intention to pursue more than one major (dual or triple major) or a graduate degree in law, criminal justice, astronomy, biology, marketing, finance, economics, or psychometrics (testing)—and then following through. Nevertheless, a high HSGPA remains important.

If your child graduates and finds himself unemployed, his degree may be in a highly competitive field where job availability is low, or he may need to relocate to another area of the state or country where job availability is higher. It could also be that his college GPA was not high enough to be hired. Once again, grades matter.

When your college-bound child is accepted to a college of his choice, it's an occasion for great joy. He is on his way to pursuing his dreams! Nevertheless, he should be made aware of two things: most schools offer core courses that must be taken before registering for any courses in his desired major, and academic departments (divisions within the school which houses the majors) usually have a GPA entrance requirement to that major/department and may not admit those with a 2.0. Many require a 3.0 or higher—another reason to have good study habits in place before going to college.

117. Provide many opportunities for your child to be a team player.

In college, instructors and professors expect team-playing skills when undertaking group assignments or projects. These skills may become imperative when a study group is needed for the course because the reading load is difficult to manage.

Starting with preschool and all through elementary, middle, and high school, encourage your child to be a team player. Participation in a team or other group—whether teacher assigned or student generated—requires the following:

- good manners
- arriving at meetings and submitting requested information on time
- sharing materials, ideas, and the floor (when speaking)
- completing one's part of a task
- knowing how to wait and take one's turn
- cooperation
- acceptance of differences of opinion
- recognition that others have strengths

- recognition that one person does not have all the answers
- ability to evaluate suggestions as well as the performance of others and oneself

Different personalities inevitably emerge within small groups and have to be dealt with in order to achieve the goal. The more positive roles are the facilitator, latent leader, and contributor, described as follows:

- The *facilitator* organizes the group, prepares materials, opens and closes meetings, prepares questions to keep the group functioning, and guides the discussion to its conclusion or consensus.
- The *latent leader* may offer constructive, helpful information or suggestions, often causing others to consider her for the leadership position in the event the leader steps down or is removed. Some latent leaders await the moment to seize the leadership position—never having said a word—which calls for a strong, outspoken member to question her ability to lead.
- The *contributor* gives information or makes corrections—a useful role, but sometimes unnerving to a few members.

Some less positive group members are the observer, who is usually quiet, shy, and may not fully participate unless called upon; the dominator/talker, who does not let others have a chance, disrupts the proceedings, and wants to be the center of attention; the introverted, shy person who rarely if ever says or volunteers for anything (she may want to, however); and the shirker or slacker, who avoids or does not do her share of the work. Group members must be willing to serve both as leader and follower when called upon.

118. Prepare your college-bound child for encounters with individuals whose values and behaviors are different from his and yours.

College exposes students to different people with dissimilar experiences, values, ideation, beliefs, and backgrounds. Often the first encounter with different personalities is in the residence hall, where the grossly untidy meet the neat freaks, the obsequiously considerate meet the obnoxiously rude, the pious meet the atheistic, and members of functional families meet members of dysfunctional families. The majority of your child's classmates, however, will fall between these extremes. College is a time during which your child may experiment and "try on" experiences. Do not panic, especially if you have given him a strong foundation.

Remind and discuss with your child your family goals and why you have them. Together as a family, you have decided that education is a priority for comfortable living, or for becoming an informed and productive citizen—whatever the family's belief about the role of education in human development and advancement. Explain to your child that in college, he will encounter some students who will be going in a direction opposite to his and will either have something to say about his decision or offer an enticement to take him off his path. If he listens to and tries their suggestions, he may lose sight of his goal.

Despite these pressures, college is a place where he and other young adults will learn how to manage their newfound independence. You must hope he will neither compromise his values nor sell his soul. Despite the stress, college is fun!

119. Encourage your child to be realistic when matching strengths to desired career.

Make your child aware that colleges offer courses of study leading to a profession, occupation, or career. Admissions officers examine a student's intended/declared major and grades in high school courses that relate to that major. For example, your high school child who graduates with a C+ average in mathematics may want to major in engineering, but entering students seeking that major need a strong mathematics foundation and proven ability because math is used extensively in engineering.

Encourage your child to talk to his high school academic counselor or the academic dean during freshman orientation about possible strategies to achieve his career goal. One suggestion may be to declare a major in the field in which he has the highest grades. If he truly wants to be an engineer, one strategy is to take all of his electives in math, starting with the lowest level math course, with the objective of earning As and transferring into the engineering program. Tell your child that Cs in his college major might as well be failing grades. Applicants with a GPA of 2.0 are often rejected by graduate and professional schools. Many graduate schools admit academically strong students, because in many graduate programs, students earning a C in any course will be dismissed. No one graduates with a grade point average less than 3.0.

If your child works throughout high school to save for college tuition and the work is negatively impacting his academic performance, the same thing may happen in college, because in all likelihood his low grades will disqualify him from academic scholarships. However, if he scores high on the SAT and/or ACT, he may be admitted and qualify for a scholarship or other forms of financial aid. Help him research scholarships specifically designed for students with any and all of his characteristics, including the following:

- HSGPA
- religion
- ethnicity
- intended major
- work record

- parents' employment field
- hobby
- disability
- sorority
- fraternity
- social club membership
- native language
- immigrant
- migrant worker
- employment
- parents' employment.

Another big help in finding a college or university that suits your child is the Peterson's guide, online at http://www.petersons. com. The guide may also be found in the reference sections of public libraries. The guide groups and describes colleges in many ways. For example, admissions difficulty (selectivity) is divided into the following categories: noncompetitive, minimally difficult, moderately difficult, very difficult, and most difficult. Cutoff scores for SAT and ACT scores and HSGPAs are listed. Colleges are also organized by state, cost, areas of study (majors), student population, degree type, and setting (urban, rural, small town, suburban).

120. If your child has a less-than-ideal GPA, help him find other ways to get accepted.

Many 2.75 and 3.0 HSGPA students assume that Ivy League schools (like Harvard, Yale, Columbia, and Princeton) are beyond their reach and never consider them as possibilities. However, the Harvard University class of 2017, with an average HSGPA of 3.83, did accept one or more students with a HSGPA of 2.68.[47] How is this possible? Students with uninspiring HSGPAs who bring to the table unique skills, talents, experiences, and accomplishments—including publications, inventions, and research projects—or have extenuating circumstances, such as a long illness or death in the family, may be admitted to the college of their choice.

There are also some well-known campuses like Drexel University—an excellent school for the sciences, especially engineering—that have numerically lower HSGPA, SAT, and ACT requirements than schools of comparable recognition. According to CollegeData, it also admitted at least one student with a 2.59 HSGPA.[48]

Assume your child will be invited to an interview that can make or break his being accepted. He should be neatly and appropriately dressed and look into the eyes of the interviewer as they speak. His handshake must be firm. Responses to the questions asked should be courteous and consistent with his previous statements. Humor may be used, but not excessively. He should be able to answer questions about his intended field of endeavor and have knowledge about the school's offerings in his field. Appropriately placed knowledge of recent trends or research in the field cannot hurt. Oftentimes, the interviewer will ask about hobbies, research interests, and travel experiences because institutions seek multifaceted, multitalented, cooperative individuals.

Your child must be prepared to speak intelligently on a few topics. Suggested areas are current events, the arts, advancements in his field of interest (major), and his passion. Entertainment—including sports—should *not* be included unless it is related to the intended field of study. For example, if your child wants to major in engineering and his passion is electronic games, a relationship between the two may be established in conversation. Yet he must not give the officer the impression that he has spent or will spend much of his time playing electronic games.

The ability to speak well in an interview is a skill every college-bound student should possess, so consider having your child take at least one public speaking course while in high school. If public speaking is not offered, Toastmasters International can help with your child's public speaking development. Toastmasters is an educational, nonprofit organization that began its trek to its international status in 1905 under the direction of Ralph C. Smedley. Since that time, Toastmasters clubs have been helping young adults improve their public speaking, communication, and leadership skills. Organized in 1930 as Toastmaster's International, it remains the widely recognized sponsor of public speaking contests.[49]

If for an unavoidable reason your child cannot attend the interview, have him call the number given in the letter, explain the circumstances, and ask if the interview can be rescheduled. Remember that the interview often determines whether the candidate will be accepted. This is when everything he has been taught over thirteen or so years comes into play—manners, speech, assertiveness, interpersonal relationships, academic and nonacademic knowledge, and personal experiences.

Related to not having the "right" HSGPA is not pursuing the right major while in college. A young woman in the last semester of her senior year in college decided she did not want to be an elementary school teacher, the field for which she had been preparing for three and a half years; instead, she wanted to be a dentist. She thought she would have to start all over again until she was advised to make an appointment with the admissions officer of the nearest school of dentistry to seek advice. After examining her transcript with a GPA of almost 4.0 and consulting with others, the officer told her that if she took and earned As in each of three science courses with labs (physics, chemistry, and organic chemistry) and earned a decent score on the Dentistry Aptitude Test (DAT), she would be admitted. The young woman earned those three As and the required score. She is now an oral surgeon. Often candidates from diverse academic backgrounds, such as an education major, make excellent graduate students because they bring to the school population different perspectives and skill sets.

121. Show your child how to maintain and safeguard his academic records.

Teachers and administrators are human, and losses do happen. Important documents in the institution's possession can be misplaced, misfiled, or lost. To protect himself, your child must learn to document his academic life. Purchase a file box or cabinet in which documents related to academics can safely be kept, including the following:

- report cards, transcripts, and evaluations
- tests and quizzes
- reports, research papers, and essays
- photographs of artwork and projects
- letters of acceptance, recommendation, and rejection
- certifications, awards, honors, medals, and commendations
- visas, passports, and birth certificate
- copies of health and immunization records
- drawings, illustrations, and musical compositions

Many of these items can be put on a jump drive to make an electronic portfolio for both possible future employment and college use.

At least one hard copy and the electronic portfolio of high school and college intellectual property should be maintained, taken to college, and kept up. It should include research papers, creative writing, and essays, especially those that earned As. These references may come in handy, and with polishing, they may be publishable.

Make sure your child does not assume his A+ high school paper will earn a decent grade in college. Chances are it will not; college writing requires depth in thought and application of knowledge from coursework as well as information learned in other courses. Additionally, the treatment of topics is neither self-centered nor shallow but global and thought-provoking, going well beyond summation and analysis to synthesis.

Notes

45 Saul Geiser and Maria Veronica Santelices, "Validity of High-School Grades in Predicting Student Success Beyond the Freshman Year: High-School Record vs. Standardized Tests as Indicators of Four-Year College Outcomes," *Center for Studies in Higher Education* 9, no. 7 (June 2007), http://www.cshe.berkeley.edu/publications/validity-high-school-grades-predicting-student-success-beyond-freshman-yearhigh-school.

46 "College Profile: University of North Carolina at Chapel Hill," CollegeData, accessed May 1, 2015, http://www.collegedata.com/cs/data/college/college_pg01_tmpl.jhtml?schoolId=1600; "College Admissions Tracker Results: Boston University," CollegeData, accessed May 1, 2015, http://www.collegedata.com/cs/admissions/admissions_tracker_result.jhtml?schoolId=146&classYear=2019; "College Admissions Tracker Results: Spelman College," CollegeData, accessed May 1, 2015, http://www.collegedata.com/cs/admissions/admissions_tracker_result.jhtml?schoolId=1659&classYear=2019; "College Admissions Tracker Results: Case Western Reserve University," CollegeData, accessed May 1, 2015, http://www.collegedata.com/cs/admissions/admissions_tracker_result.jhtml?schoolId=966&classYear=2019; "College Admissions Tracker Results: Howard University," CollegeData, accessed May 1, 2015, http://www.collegedata.com/cs/admissions/admissions_tracker_result.jhtml?schoolId=1024&classYear=2019); "College Admissions Tracker Results: Harvard College," accessed May 1, 2015, http://www.collegedata.com/cs/admissions/admissions_tracker_result.jhtml?schoolId=444&classYear=2019; "College Admissions Tracker Results: Mary Baldwin College," CollegeData, accessed May 1, 2015, http://www.collegedata.com/cs/admissions/admissions_tracker_result.jhtml?schoolId=898&classYear=2019.

47 "College Admissions Tracker Results: Harvard College," CollegeData, accessed May 1, 2015, http://www.collegedata.com/cs/admissions/admissions_tracker_result.jhtml?schoolId=444&classYear=2019.

48 "College Admissions Tracker Results: Drexel University," CollegeData, accessed May 1, 2015, http://www.collegedata.com/cs/admissions/admissions_tracker_result.jhtml?schoolId=407&classYear=2019.

49 Toastmaster's International, accessed May 1, 2015, https://www.toastmasters.org.

CONCLUDING REMARKS

While the experts rethink, reconsider, revise, and revamp education, parents—the most visibly absent part of the present educational process—are finding ways to address their children's problems in literacy, mathematics, technology, and study skills. I hope that you have identified in this work a range of options to help you create a holistic, focused, and practicable plan of action to improve your child's overall academic experiences and performance. Equipped to be proactive in the education of your child, you join a growing movement of hundreds of thousands of parents across the nation committed to the fight for and protection of their children's futures. Parents are the most motivated to effectively intervene because of their undying love for their children and the unique control they are able to exercise over their children.

It is our view that each child is a national asset to be protected, nurtured, groomed, and well educated regardless of socioeconomic status, ethnicity, race, culture, nationality, or sexual persuasion. Reasons for this position are the aging of America; the precipitous decline of the farming and manufacturing industries; the growing domestic and international economies dependent on individuals proficient in mathematics, science, technology, and communications; and the opportunities offered by new frontiers surrounding the environment, outer space, technology, medicine, and retirees.

Be on the lookout for forthcoming works to further help you improve your child's reading comprehension, study skills, and mathematics. We wish you much success with each of your children so that you may experience the peace of mind you eagerly desire and deserve. We would appreciate your feedback.

INDEX

Printed in the United States
By Bookmasters